Administering Windows Server® 2012 R2 Exam 70-411

Lab Manual

Patrick Regan

WILEY

EXECUTIVE EDITOR	John Kane
EDITORIAL ASSISTANT	Allison Winkle
EXECUTIVE MARKETING MANAGER	Chris Ruel
SENIOR PRODUCTION & MANUFACTURING MANAGER	Janis Soo
ASSOCIATE PRODUCTION MANAGER	Joyce Poh

www.wiley.com/college/microsoft

or

call the MOAC Toll-Free Number: 888-764-7001 (U.S. & Canada only)

ISBN   978-1-118-88291-7

Printed in the United States of America

BRIEF CONTENTS

CONTENTS

LAB 1
DEPLOYING AND MANAGING SERVER IMAGES

THIS LAB CONTAINS THE FOLLOWING EXERCISES AND ACTIVITIES:

Exercise 1.1   Installing and Configuring Windows Deployment Services

Exercise 1.2   Creating Windows Deployment Images

Exercise 1.3   Generating an Autounattend.xml file

Exercise 1.4   Deploying a Windows Image

Exercise 1.5   Updating a Windows Image

Lab Challenge   Adding Drivers to a Windows Image

BEFORE YOU BEGIN

The lab environment consists of student workstations connected to a local area network, along with a server that functions as the domain controller for a domain called *contoso.com*. The computers required for this lab are listed in Table 1-1.

Table 1-1
Computers Required for Lab 1

Computer	Operating System	Computer Name
Server (VM 1)	Windows Server 2012 R2	RWDC01
Server (VM 2)	Windows Server 2012 R2	Server01
Server (VM 3)	Windows Server 2012 R2	Server02

In addition to the computers, you also require the software listed in Table 1-2 to complete Lab 1.

Table 1-2
Software Required for Lab 1

Software	Location
ISO of Windows Server 2012 R2 installation disk	\\rwdc01\Software
Windows Assessment and Deployment Kit (ADK) for Windows 8.1	\\rwdc01\Software
Autounattend.xml file	\\rwdc01\Software
Windows8.1-KB2901549-x64.msu	\\rwdc01\Software
Lab 1 student worksheet	Lab01_worksheet.docx (provided by instructor)

Working with Lab Worksheets

Each lab in this manual requires that you answer questions, take screen shots, and perform other activities that you will document in a worksheet named for the lab, such as Lab01_worksheet.docx. You will find these worksheets on the book companion site. It is recommended that you use a USB flash drive to store your worksheets so you can submit them to your instructor for review. As you perform the exercises in each lab, open the appropriate worksheet file using Word, fill in the required information, and save the file to your flash drive.

After completing this lab, you will be able to:

- Install and configure Windows Deployment Services

- Deploy Windows servers using Windows Deployment Services

- Create and modify an Autounattend.xml file using Windows System Image Manager

- Update an offline Windows image

Estimated lab time: 100 minutes

Exercise 1.1	Installing and Configuring Windows Deployment Services
Overview	In this exercise, you will first create a new server and then install and configure Windows Deployment Services so that you can quickly install Windows servers in the future.
Mindset	You need to first install and configure a WDS server. You then need to add at least one boot and install image. You will then need to perform a PXE boot with the WDS boot image and perform the installation with the install image.
Completion time	10 minutes

1. Log into Server01 as contoso\administrator with the password of Pa$$w0rd.

2. On Server01, using the Server Manager console, click Manage > Add Roles and Features.

3. On the Add Roles and Features Wizard page, click Next.

4. On the Select installation type page, click Next.

5. On the Select destination server page, click Next.

6. Scroll down and select Windows Deployment Services.

7. On the Add Roles and Features Wizard page, click Add Features and then click Next.

8. On the Select features page, click Next.

9. On the WDS page, click Next.

10. On the Select role services page, make sure that the Deployment Server option is selected and the Transport Server option is selected and then click Next.

11. On the Confirm installation selections page, click Install.

12. When the installation finishes, click Close.

13. In Server Manager, click Tools > Windows Deployment Services. The Windows Deployment Services console opens.

14. Expand Servers. Right-click the Server01.contoso.com and choose Configure Server.

15. On the Before You Begin page, click Next.

16. On the Install Options page, select the Integrated with Active Directory option and then click Next.

17. On the Remote Installation Folder Location page, take a screen shot by pressing Alt+Prt Scr and then paste it into your Lab01_worksheet file in the page provided by pressing Ctrl+V.

18. On the Remote Installation page, answer Questions 1 and 2 that follow and then click Next.

Question 1	What is the default path for the remote installation folder?

Question 2	Why is the default location not recommended?

19. When the system volume warning appears, click Yes.

20. On the PXE Server Initial Settings page, select Respond to all client computers (known and unknown) and then click Next.

21. When the task is completed, click to deselect Add images to the server now.

22. Take a screen shot of the Windows Deployment Services Configuration Wizard page by pressing Alt+Prt Scr and then paste it into your Lab01_worksheet file in the page provided by pressing Ctrl+V.

23. Click Finish.

End of exercise. Leave Windows Deployment Services open for the next exercise.

Exercise 1.2	Creating Windows Deployment Images
Overview	In this exercise, you will prepare images (boot images and install images) that will be used to deploy Windows.
Mindset	WDS uses two images to deploy Windows. The boot image is used to boot the computer, so that the installation can be started. The install image is used to perform the actual Windows installation.
Completion time	20 minutes

1. On Server01, create a C:\Software folder.

2. On Server01, right-click the Start button, choose Run, type **\\RWDC01\Software**, and then click OK.

3. Copy the ISO file for the Windows Server 2012 R2 installation disk, the autounattend.xml file, and the Windows8.1-KB2901549-x64.msu file to the C:\Software folder.

4. On Server01, open the C:\Software folder.

5. Right-click the ISO file for Windows Server 2012 R2 installation disk and choose Mount.

Question 3	*What drive letter was the ISO file mounted to?*

6. From the Windows Deployment Services console, expand Servers and then expand Server01.contoso.com so that you can see the Install Images folder and the Boot Images folder.

7. To add a boot image, right-click the Boot Images folder and choose Add Boot Image. The Add Image Wizard opens.

Question 4	*What is the boot image based on?*

8. Browse to the E:\Sources folder, click the boot.wim file, and then click Open. Click Next.

9. On the Image Metadata page, click Next.

10. On the Summary page, click Next.

11. When the image is added to the server, click Finish.

12. Right-click the Install Images folder and choose Add Install Image. The Add Image Wizard page opens.

13. On the Image Group page, the Create an image group named option is selected. Click Next.

14. Browse to the E:\Sources folder, double-click the install.wim file and then click Next.

15. On the Available Images page (as shown on Figure 1-1), deselect the following images:

- Windows Server 2012 R2 SERVERSTANDARDCORE
- Windows Server 2012 R2 SERVERDATACENTERCORE
- Windows Server 2012 R2 SERVERDATACENTER

Be sure that Windows Server 2012 R2 SERVERSTANDARD (second option) is selected.

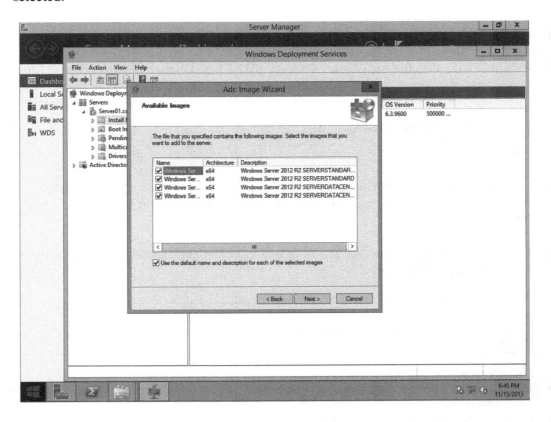

Figure 1-1
Selecting images to use

16. Click Next.

17. On the Summary page, click Next.

18. When the image is added to the server, click Finish.

19. Take a screen shot of the Windows Deployment Services Add Image Wizard page by pressing Alt+Prt Scr and then paste it into your Lab 1 worksheet file in the page provided by pressing Ctrl+V.

End of exercise. You can leave any windows open for the next exercise.

Exercise 1.3	Generating an Autounattend.xml File
Overview	You are ready to deploy Windows. However, if you install using WDS, you will have to interact with the Windows installation program by choosing applicable settings during the installation process. To help automate the installation, in this exercise, you will create an Autoattend.xml file and then check a provided Autounattend.xml file.
Mindset	You need to create an unattended xml file and then you need to configure the WDS server to use the Unattended.xml file. When configuring the unattended file, it must be configured to include each prompt during the installation process.
Completion time	20 minutes

1. On Server01, right-click the Start button, choose Run, type **\\rwdc01\software**, and then click OK. Copy the ADK folder to the C:\Software folder.

2. Open the E:\Sources folder and copy the install.wim file to the C:\Software folder.

3. On Server01, open the C:\Software\ADK folder.

Question 5	*What are the two ways to create or modify an unattend xml file?*

4. To start the installation of the Windows Assessment and Deployment Kit, double-click adksetup.exe. If you are prompted to confirm that you want to run this file, click Run.

5. On the Specify Location page, leave the default settings and then click Next.

6. When you are prompted to join the Customer Experience Improvement Program (CEIP), click Next.

7. On the License Agreement page, click Accept.

8. Deselect all options except Deployment Tools and Windows Preinstallation Environment (Windows PE). Click Install.

9. When the installation is complete, click Close.

10. Using Windows Explorer, create a folder named C:\DistFold.

11. Click Start > Apps (down arrow) > Windows System Image Manager. The Windows System Image Manager console opens.

12. Click Tools > Create Distribution Share. The Create Distribution Share dialog box opens.

13. In the Folder name text box, type **C:\DistFold** folder and then click Open.

14. Click File > Select Windows Image. The Select a Windows Image dialog box opens.

15. In the File name text box, type **C:\Software\install.wim** and then click Open. Click Windows Server 2012 R2 SERVERSTANDARD and then click OK.

16. If you are prompted to create a catalog file, click Yes.

17. Click File > New Answer File. The answer file elements display in the Answer File pane.

18. In the Windows Image pane, expand Components. Scroll down and right-click amd64_Microsoft-Windows-International-Core-WinPE_6. 3.9600. 16384_neutral and choose Add Setting to Pass 1 windowsPE, as shown in Figure 1-2.

Figure 1-2
Adding Settings to Pass 1 WindowsPE

The Microsoft-Windows-International-Core-WinPE component specifies the default language, locale, and other international settings to use during Windows Setup or Windows Deployment Services installations.

19. In the Answer File pane, click amd64_Microsoft-Windows-International-Core-WinPE_neutral. Complete the language settings (as shown in Figure 1-3) as appropriate, such as en-US.

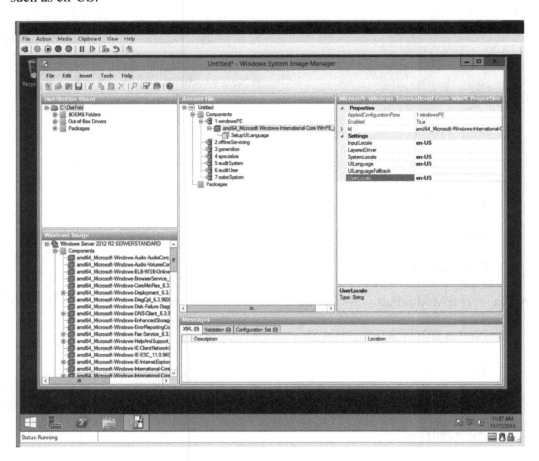

Figure 1-3
Specifying language settings

20. Expand amd64_Microsoft-Windows-International-Core-WinPE_neutral and click SetupUILanguage. In the properties for UILanguage, type en-US.

   The Microsoft-Windows-Setup component contains settings that enable you to select the Windows image that you install, configure the disk that you install Windows to, and configure the Windows PE operating system.

21. In the Windows Image pane, right-click amd64_Microsoft-Windows-Setup_6.3.9600.16384_neutral and choose Add Setting to Pass 1 windowsPE.

22. In the Answer File pane, expand amd64_Microsoft-Windows-Setup_neutral, right-click DiskConfiguration, and choose Insert New Disk.

23. In the Answer File pane, expand amd64_Microsoft-Windows-Setup_neutral, expand Disk, right-click CreatePartitions, and choose Insert New CreatePartition.

24. Specify an order of 1, a size of 350, and a type of Primary.

25. Right-click CreatePartitions and choose Insert New CreatePartition. For the new CreatePartition entry, change the Extend property to true and set Order to 2. Don't configure the size.

26. In the Answer File pane, click Disk. Change the DiskID to 0 and change WillWipeDisk to true.

27. Right-click ModifyPartitions and choose Insert New ModifyPartition. Then specify the following:

       Active is true

       Format is NTFS

       Label is Boot

       Order is 1

       PartitionID is 1

28. Add a second ModifyPartitions and configure as the following:

       Format is NTFS

       Label is System

       Order is 2

       PartitionID is 2

29. In the Answer File pane, scroll down to and expand ImageInstall and then expand OSImage. Right-click InstallFrom and choose Insert New Metadata. Configure the metadata as shown Figure 1-4.

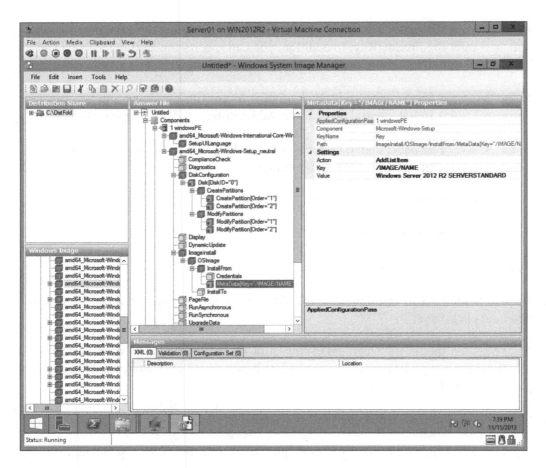

Figure 1-4
Specifying which image to use

30. Click InstallTo and then configure the DiskID to 0 and PartitionID to 2.

31. In the Answer File pane, click UserData and then specify the following:

    Accept EULA is true

    FullName is Student

    Organization is Classroom

32. Expand UserData and then click ProductKey. If you have a key, type the Windows key in the Key box. For this lab, leave it blank.

    Microsoft-Windows-Shell-Setup contains elements and settings that control how the shell of the Windows operating system is installed on a destination computer.

33. In the Windows Image pane, right-click amd64_Microsoft-Windows-Shell-Setup_6.3.9600.16404_neutral and choose Add Settings to Pass 4 specialize.

34. In the Answer File pane, click amd64_Microsoft-Windows-Shell-Setup_neutral. Here, you also enter the ProductKey. In addition, you can specify the ComputerName and TimeZone. For now, leave these blank.

35. In the Windows Image pane, right-click amd64_Microsoft-Windows-Shell-Setup_6.3.9600.16404_neutral and choose Add Settings to Pass 7 oobeSystem.

36. In the Answer File pane, under 7 oobeSystem/amd64_Microsoft-Windows-Shell-Setup_neutral, configure the following settings:

Registered Organization is Classroom

Registered Owner is Student

37. Click File > Save Answer File.

38. Browse to the C:\Software folder. In the File name text box, type Unattend (Temp).xml and then click Save.

39. Take a screen shot of the Unattend (Temp).xml - Windows System Image Manager screen by pressing Alt+Prt Scr and then paste it into your Lab 1 worksheet file in the page provided by pressing Ctrl+V.

40. Click File > Close Answer File.

41. On Server01, using Windows System Image Manager, click File > Open Answer File. In the C:\Software folder, click the autounattend.xml file and then click Open.

Question 6	You downloaded an autounattend.xml file from the Internet and you made some changes. What is the best way to validate the file?

42. Click Tools > Validate Answer File.

43. In the Messages pane, make sure there are no errors. Warnings will appear; they are common.

44. Take a screen shot of the autounattend.xml - Windows System Image Manager screen by pressing Alt+Prt Scr and then paste it into your Lab01_worksheet file in the page provided by pressing Ctrl+V.

45. In the Answer File pane, expand the structure and view the various settings.

46. Close Windows System Image Manager.

47. Open the C:\Software folder.

48. Right-click the autounattend.xml file, choose Open with, and choose Notepad.

49. Scroll through the document and review the various settings.

50. Close Notepad.

End of exercise. You can leave any windows open for the next exercise.

Exercise 1.4	Deploying a Windows Image
Overview	In this exercise, you will deploy a Windows image from the WDS server while using the autounattended.xml file.
Mindset	By default, if you deploy Windows images using WDS, you will still be performing a manual installation over the network if you do not specify and configure autounattend.xml files.
Completion time	10 minutes

1. On Server01, copy the C:\Software\autounattend.xml file to the C:\RemoteInstall folder.

2. If Windows Deployment Services is not open, on the Server Manager console, click Tools > Windows Deployment Services. The Windows Deployment Services console opens.

3. Expand Servers. Then right-click Server01.contoso.com and choose Properties. The server's Properties dialog box opens.

4. Click the Client tab.

5. Select the Enable unattended installation check box. Click the Browse button corresponding to the x64 architecture, browse to C:\RemoteInstall\autounattend.xml, and then click Open. When completed, the Font: regular tab should look like Figure 1-5.

Question 7	*If you have a mix of 32-bit and 64-bit versions of Windows, which architectures should you add a unattended installation file for?*

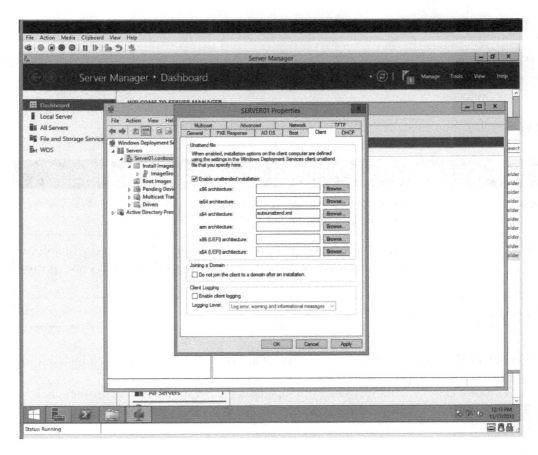

Figure 1-5
Configuring the Client settings

6. Click OK to close the server's Properties sheet.

7. Expand the Server01.contoso.com node, expand the Install Images node, and then click ImageGroup1.

8. Right-click the Windows Server 2012 R2 SERVERSTANDARD image and choose Properties. The Image Properties dialog box opens.

9. Click to select the Allow image to install in unattended mode check box.

10. Click Select File. The Select Unattend File dialog box opens.

11. Browse to C:\RemoteInstall\autounattend.xml, click Open, and then click OK.

12. Take a screen shot of the Image Properties dialog box by pressing Alt+Prt Scr and then paste it into your Lab01_worksheet file in the page provided by pressing Ctrl+V.

13. Click OK to accept your settings and to close the Image Properties dialog box.

You are now ready to perform a PXE boot on a new server and perform an installation of Windows Server 2012 R2.

End of exercise. Close Windows Deployment Services and any Explorer folders that are open.

Exercise 1.5	Updating a Windows Image
Overview	From time to time, you need to patch a Windows image. In this execise, you will add a Windows update package to the install.wim file.
Mindset	When you update an installation image using the Dism command, the Windows package must be a cabinet (.cab) file or a Windows Update Stand-alone Installation (.msu) file.
Completion time	20 minutes

1. On Server01, create a C:\Package folder.

2. Create a C:\Offline folder.

3. Right-click the Start button and choose Command Prompt (Admin).

4. To change to the C:\Software folder, execute the following command at the command prompt:

   ```
   cd\Software
   ```

5. To extract the cab files from the Windows8.1-KB2901549-x64.msu file, execute the following command:

   ```
   Windows8.1-KB2901549-x64.msu /extract:C:\Package
   ```

6. Using Windows Explorer, view the content of the Font: regular folder.

7. Take a screen shot of the Package folder by pressing Alt+Prt Scr and then paste it into your Lab01_worksheet file in the page provided by pressing Ctrl+V.

8. Open Windows Deployment Services.

9. Navigate to the ImageGroup1 node, which is under Install Images.

10. In the ImageGroup1 pane, right-click the Windows Server 2012 R2 SERVERSTANDARD image and choose Disable.

11. Right-click the Windows Server 2012 R2 SERVERSTANDARD image and choose Export Image.

12. In the Export As dialog box, in the File name text box, type **C:\Software\install.wim** and then click Save. If you are prompted to confirm that you want to continue, click Yes.

Question 8	*What is the first step that you have to perform before you can add a Windows package to a WIM file?*

13. In the Administrator: Command Prompt window, to mount the c:\Software\install.wim file, execute the following command:

```
dism /Mount-Wim /WimFile:C:\Software\install.wim /index:1
/MountDir:C:\Offline
```

14. To get information about the WIM file, execute the following command:

```
dism /Get-WimInfo /WimFile:C:\software\install.wim /index:1
```

15. To add the package to the WIM image, execute the following command:

```
dism /image:C:\Offline /Add-Package
/Packagepath:C:\Package\Windows8.1-KB2901549-x64.cab
```

16. To commit the changes to the WIM file, execute the following command:

```
dism /Commit-Wim /MountDir:C:\Offline
```

17. To dismount the WIM file, execute the following command:

```
dism /Unmount-Wim /MountDir:C:\Offline /commit
```

18. Take a screen shot of the Command Prompt by pressing Alt+Prt Scr and then paste it into your Lab01_worksheet file in the page provided by pressing Ctrl+V.

19. Go back to Windows Deployment Services console.

20. Right-click the Windows Server 2012 R2 SERVERSTANDARD image and choose Replace Image.

21. On the Replace Install Image Wizard page, use the Browse button to browse to the C:\Software\install.wim file and then click Next.

22. On the Available Images page, click Next.

23. On the Image Metadata page, click Next.

24. On the Summary page, click Next.

25. When the image is replaced, click Finish. The image is automatically enabled.

26. Close the Administrator: Command Prompt window and close Windows Deployment Services.

End of exercise. Close all windows.

LAB REVIEW QUESTIONS

Completion time	10 minutes

1. In Exercise 1.1, what program did you use to install WDS?

2. In Exercise 1.2, what two images did you have to add to the WDS server to handle the Windows installation?

3. In Exercise 1.3, what program did you use to create the unattend file?

4. In Exercise 1.3, what program should you use to verify a unattend file?

5. In Exercise 1.3, how was the Windows System Image Manager installed?

6. In Exercise 1.4, what two places did you have to define an unattend file?

7. In Exercise 1.5, what program did you use to modify a Windows image?

Lab Challenge	Adding Drivers to a Windows Image
Overview	To complete this challenge, you must demonstrate how to add drivers to a Windows image by writing the steps to complete the tasks described in the scenerio. Since the class servers do not have drivers to add, just write the steps as if the drivers actually existed.
Mindset	Over the last couple of months, you have been using WDS to deploy Windows Server 2012 R2. Recently, you started to purchase new servers that require additional drivers that are not included with the Windows installation. You need to ensure that WDS will deploy these drivers. You need to explain how to add drivers to a Windows image.
Completion time	10 minutes

Write out the steps you performed to complete the challenge.

End of lab.

LAB 2
IMPLEMENTING PATCH MANAGEMENT

BEFORE YOU BEGIN

The lab environment consists of student workstations connected to a local area network, along with a server that functions as the domain controller for a domain called *contoso.com*. The computers required for this lab are listed in Table 2-1.

Table 2-1
Computers Required for Lab 2

Computer	Operating System	Computer Name
Server (VM 1)	Windows Server 2012 R2	RWDC01
Server (VM 2)	Windows Server 2012 R2	Server01
Server (VM 3)	Windows Server 2012 R2	Server02

In addition to the computers, you also require the software listed in Table 2-2 to complete Lab 2.

Table 2-2
Software Required for Lab 2

Software	Location
Lab 2 student worksheet	Lab02_worksheet.docx (provided by instructor)

Working with Lab Worksheets

Each lab in this manual requires that you answer questions, take screen shots, and perform other activities that you will document in a worksheet named for the lab, such as Lab02_worksheet.docx. You will find these worksheets on the book companion site. It is recommended that you use a USB flash drive to store your worksheets so you can submit them to your instructor for review. As you perform the exercises in each lab, open the appropriate worksheet file using Word, fill in the required information, and save the file to your flash drive.

After completing this lab, you will be able to:

- Install and configure WSUS

- Deploy updates to client computers

Estimated lab time: 60 minutes

Exercise 2.1	Installing WSUS
Overview	In this exercise, you will use Server Manager to install WSUS. Because this is a test environment, you use the standard internal database that comes with Windows.
Mindset	When planning WSUS, you should consider the number of clients, number of updates, location of the clients, bandwidth links between the clients and the WSUS server, and available disk space. If you have multiple sites, you might consider installing multiple WSUS servers within your organization so that you can preserve WAN bandwidth. You can then consider using a WSUS architecture.
Completion time	10 minutes

1. Log into Server01 as contoso\administrator with the password of Pa$$w0rd.

2. Using File Explorer, create a C:\Updates folder.

3. To deploy WSUS, Network Services needs to have Full Control to the %windir%\Microsoft.NET\Framework\v2.0.50727\Temporary ASP.NET Files and %windir%\Temp folder. Open the %windir% folder.

Question 1	*What folder does the %windir% folder represent?*

4. Right-click the Temp folder and select Properties.

5. In the Temp Properties dialog box, click the Security tab.

6. Click the Edit button.

7. In the Permissions for Temp folder, click Add.

8. In the Select Users, Computers, Service Accounts, or Groups dialog box, type **network service** in the Enter the object names to select text box and press Enter.

9. While NETWORK SERVICE is selected, click the Allow Full control.

10. Take a screen shot of the Permissions for Temp dialog box by pressing Alt+Prt Scr and then paste it into your Lab02_worksheet file in the page provided by pressing Ctrl+V.

11. Click OK to close the Permissions for Temp dialog box. If you are prompted to confirm that you want to change the permissions settings on system folders, click Yes.

12. Click OK to close the Temp Properties dialog box.

13. If Server Manager is not open, open Server Manager. At the top of Server Manager, click Manage > Add Roles and Features. The Add Roles and Feature Wizard displays.

14. On the Before you begin page, click Next.

15. Select Role-based or feature-based installation and then click Next.

16. On the Select destination server page, click Next.

17. Scroll down and select Windows Server Update Services.

18. In the Add Roles and Features Wizard, click Add Features.

19. Back on the Select server roles screen, click Next.

20. On the Select features page, click Next.

21. On the Windows Server Update Services page, click Next.

22. By default, WID Database and WSUS Services are selected as shown in Figure 2-1. Answer the following question and then click Next.

Question 2	What option would you choose in order to store the database on a dedicated SQL server?

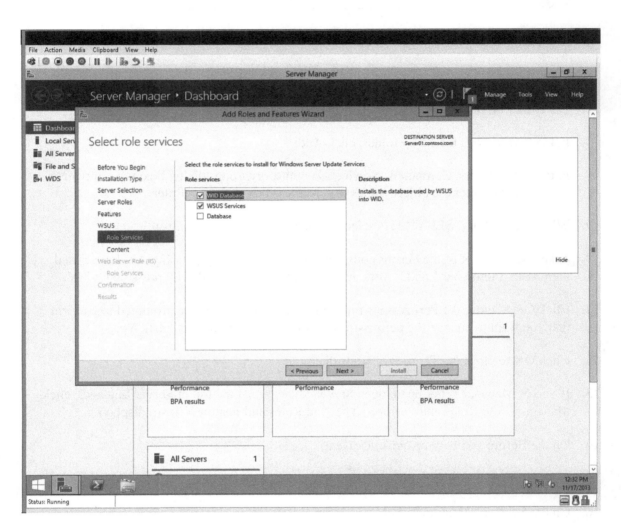

Figure 2-1
Selecting the WSUS components

23. In the Current Location text box, type **C:\Updates** and then click Next.

NOTE	Remember, if this was a production environment, you would store the updates on a non-system drive.

24. On the Web Server Role (IIS) page, click Next.

25. On the Select Role services page, click Next.

26. On the Confirm installation selections page, click Install.

27. When the installation has completed, take a screen shot of the Add Roles and Features Wizard by pressing Alt+Prt Scr and then paste it into your Lab 2 worksheet file in the page provided by pressing Ctrl+V.

28. Click Close.

End of exercise. You can leave the windows open for the next exercise.

Exercise 2.2	Configuring WSUS
Overview	After you install WSUS, you must configure WSUS so that it retrieves updates from Microsoft or another WSUS server. You also need to configure WSUS on what updates need to be downloaded and when the downloads should occur.
Mindset	After the WSUS server has been installed, it must be configured so that it knows where to get the updates from and what to download. If your office or school uses a proxy server to access the Internet, you will need to input the proxy settings so that WSUS can get to the Internet and Microsoft's websites. This would include specifying the name or IP address for the actual server or device and the appropriate port that all Internet traffic must flow through to reach the Internet.
Completion time	20 minutes

1. On Server01, if Server Manager is not open, open Server Manager.

2. At the top of Server Manager, click Tools > Windows Server Update Services.

3. In the Complete WSUS Installation dialog box, click Run.

4. When the post-installation successfully is completed, take a screen shot of the Complete WSUS Installation dialog box by pressing Alt+Prt Scr and then paste it into your Lab 2 worksheet file in the page provided by pressing Ctrl+V.

5. Click Close.

6. On the Before You Begin page, click Next.

7. On the Join the Microsoft Update Improvement Program page, clear the Yes, I would like to join the Microsoft Update Improvement Program check box, then click Next.

8. The Choose Upstream Server page displays. Click Synchronize from another Windows Server Update Services server. In the Server name text box, type **server02.contoso.com**. Answer the following question and then click Next.

Question 3	*After synchronizing from another WSUS server, what default port is used?*

9. On the Specify Proxy Server page, click Next.

10. On the Connect to Upstream Server page, click Start Connecting.

11. When the connection is complete, click Next.

12. On the Choose Languages page, choose one language that you need to support and then click Next.

NOTE	*If you were updating directly from Microsoft, you would choose which products and which classifications to download. However, because you are downloading from another WSUS server, you automatically get the products and classifications used on the upstream server.*

13. On the Set Sync Schedule page (see Figure 2-2), click Next.

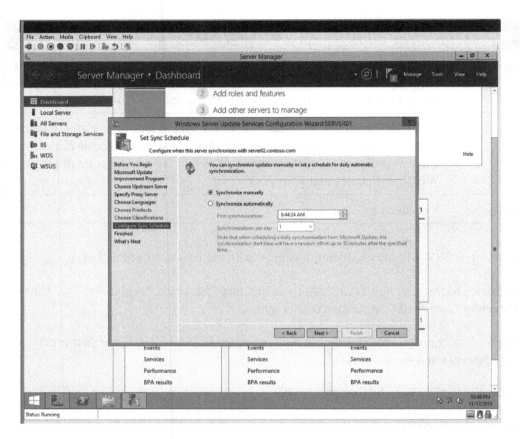

Figure 2-2
Specifying when to sync updates

14. On the Finished page, select Begin initial synchronization and then click Next.

15. On the What's Next page, click Finish.

16. On the WSUS console, expand Server01 and then click Synchronizations.

17. Take a screen shot of the Update Services console by pressing Alt+Prt Scr and then paste it into your Lab02_worksheet file in the page provided by pressing Ctrl+V.

18. Synchronization should already be running. Go to the Update Services console and at the bottom of the left pane, click Options to show the WSUS options. View the available options.

19. In the left pane, expand Computers so that you can see All Computers.

20. Right-click All Computers and choose Add Computer Group. The Add Computer Group dialog box opens.

21. In the Name text box, type **Group1**. Click Add to apply your settings and to close the Add Computer Group dialog box.

End of exercise. You can leave the windows open for the next exercise.

Exercise 2.3	Configuring Clients
Overview	For a client to get updates from a WSUS, the client has to be configured to get updates from WSUS. Therefore, during this exercise, you will use group policies to configure Server02 to get updates from Server01.
Mindset	You have hundreds of clients that need to get Windows updates. Rather than configure each computer one-by-one, what would be the easiest way to configure all of the computers so that the computers will get the Windows updates that you specify?
Completion time	5 minutes

1. Log into RWDC01 as contoso\administrator with the password of Pa$$w0rd.

2. In Server Manager, click Tools > Active Directory Users and Computers. The Active Directory Users and Computers console opens.

3. Right-click contoso.com and choose New > Organizational Unit. In the Name text box, type **Servers** and then click OK.

4. Navigate to and click the Computers OU.

5. Right-click Server02 and choose Move.

6. Select Servers and click OK.

7. Close Active Directory Users and Computers.

8. In Server Manager, click Tools > Group Policy Management. The Group Policy Management console opens.

9. In the tree structure (left pane), expand Forests: contoso.com, expand Domains, expand contoso.com and click Servers.

10. Right-click Servers and chose Create a GPO in this domain, and Link it here.

11. In the New GPO dialog box, in the Name text box, type **Server Updates** and then click OK.

12. Expand the Servers node so that you can view the Server Updates GPO. Right-click the Servers Update GPO, and then choose Edit. The Group Policy Management Editor opens.

13. In Group Policy Management Editor, expand Computer Configuration > Policies > Administrative Templates > Windows Components and click Windows Update, as shown in Figure 2-3.

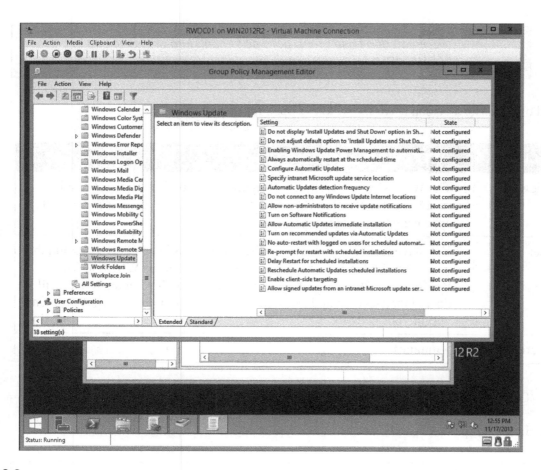

Figure 2-3
Viewing the Windows update options in a GPO

14. In the details pane, double-click Specify intranet Microsoft update service location.

15. Select Enabled.

16. In the Set the intranet update service for detecting updates text box and in the Set the intranet statistics server text box, type **HTTP://Server01:8530**.

17. Click OK to apply your settings and to close the Specify intranet Microsoft update service location page.

18. In the details pane, double-click Enable client-side targeting. The Enable client-side targeting page appears.

19. Select Enabled and in the Target group name for this computer text box, type **Group1**.

20. Take a screen shot of the Enable client-side targeting page by pressing Alt+Prt Scr and then paste it into your Lab 2 worksheet file in the page provided by pressing Ctrl+V.

21. Click OK to apply your settings and to close the Enable client-side targeting page.

Question 4	*If you don't use group policies to configure clients to use WSUS, how would you configure the system?*

End of exercise. You can leave the windows open for the next exercise.

Exercise 2.4	Approving Updates
Overview	The WSUS server has been configured and you have a client that is ready to get updates from the WSUS server. In this exercise, you will approve what updates need to be pushed.
Mindset	You have just configured the WSUS server has been configured and the clients have been configured to get updates from the WSUS server. Before you approve updates, You should research what an update will do and then test the update thoroughly so that it does not cause problems within your network.
Completion time	5 minutes

1. On Server01, go to the Update Services console.

2. In the left pane, expand Server01, click Updates.

Question 5	*Why is the Updates needed by computers option not available?*

3. In the Critical Updates section, click Updates installed/not applicable.

4. On the top of the screen, in the Approval drop-down, make sure Unapproved is selected. On the top of the screen, on the Status drop-down menu, make sure Any is selected (as shown in Figure 2-4).

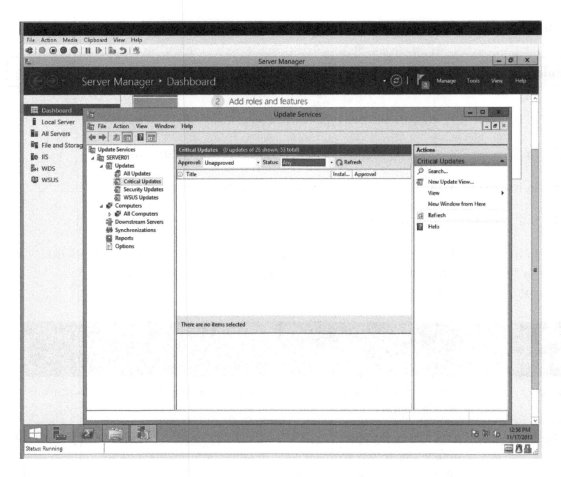

Figure 2-4
Showing unapproved updates

5. Click Refresh to display the updates.

6. To click several updates, hold the Ctrl key and click several updates. When you're finished selecting your updates, release the Ctrl key.

7. Right-click the selected updates and choose Approve.

8. If the Approve Updates dialog box displays, select the Group1 drop down arrow and choose Approved For Install. Click OK.

9. If a license agreement displays, prompting you for an update, click I Accept.

10. Take a screen shot of the Update Services console by pressing Alt+Prt Scr and then paste it into your Lab 2 worksheet file in the page provided by pressing Ctrl+V.

11. Click Close.

End of exercise. Close all windows.

LAB REVIEW QUESTIONS

Completion time	10 minutes

1. In Exercise 2.1, what are the two types of databases that WSUS supports?

2. In Exercise 2.2, what two sources can a WSUS server get updates from?

3. In Exercise 2.3, in WSUS, how do you specify which computers get updates?

4. In Exercise 2.3, what is the easiest way to configure the clients to use a WSUS server?

5. In Exercise 2.3, by default, what is the HTTP specifier and what is the HTTPS URL for WSUS running on Server01. Hint: Look at the IIS Bindings for the WSUS Administration website in IIS.

Lab Challenge	Running WSUS Reports
Overview	To complete this challenge, you will describe the steps needed to run WSUS reports.
Mindset	You have configured WSUS and the WSUS clients. You have approved updates yesterday and you want to know how the updates are progressing. What do you need to do to view the reports?
Completion time	10 minutes

Write out the steps you performed to complete the challenge.

End of lab.

LAB 3
MONITORING SERVERS

THIS LAB CONTAINS THE FOLLOWING EXERCISES AND ACTIVITIES:

Exercise 3.1   Using Event Viewer

Exercise 3.2   Using Reliability Monitor

Exercise 3.3   Using Task Manager

Exercise 3.4   Using Resource Monitor

Exercise 3.5   Using Performance Monitor

Exercise 3.6   Monitoring VMs

Lab Challenge   Using Network Monitor

BEFORE YOU BEGIN

The lab environment consists of student workstations connected to a local area network, along with a server that functions as the domain controller for a domain called *contoso.com*. The computers required for this lab are listed in Table 3-1.

Table 3-1
Computers Required for Lab 3

Computer	Operating System	Computer Name
Server (VM 1)	Windows Server 2012 R2	RWDC01
Server (VM 2)	Windows Server 2012 R2	Server01
Server (VM 3)	Windows Server 2012 R2	Server02

In addition to the computers, you also require the software listed in Table 3-2 to complete Lab 3.

Table 3-2
Software Required for Lab 3

Software	Location
Lab 3 student worksheet	Lab03_worksheet.docx (provided by instructor)

Working with Lab Worksheets

Each lab in this manual requires that you answer questions, take screen shots, and perform other activities that you will document in a worksheet named for the lab, such as Lab03_worksheet.docx. You will find these worksheets on the book companion site. It is recommended that you use a USB flash drive to store your worksheets so you can submit them to your instructor for review. As you perform the exercises in each lab, open the appropriate worksheet file using Word, fill in the required information, and save the file to your flash drive.

After completing this lab, you will be able to:

- Use Event Viewer to troubleshoot and monitor servers

- Use Reliability Monitor to monitor the reliability of a server

- Use Task Manager and Performance Monitor to monitor the performance of a server

Estimated lab time: 120 minutes

Exercise 3.1	Using Event Viewer
Overview	In this exercise, you will use Event Viewer to view the events stored in the Windows logs. Because there can be thousands of log entires, you will learn how to filter the logs so you can concentrate on what you need to focus on and you will learn how to set up subscriptions to consolidate the logs onto one server.
Mindset	Traditional log files give an administrator insight on what a system or program is doing or insight into any errors that might have occurred. The traditional log file is a simple text file, usually with a filename extension of log. In Windows, the logs are displayed within the Event Viewer. The Event Viewer allows you to filter the logs so that you can focus on what is relevant to the current problem or action that you are looking into.
Completion time	20 minutes

Viewing Events

1. Log into Server01 as contoso\administrator with the password Pa$$w0rd. The Server Manager console opens.

2. Click Tools > Event Viewer. The Event Viewer console opens.

3. Expand the Windows Logs folder and click the System log. The contents of the log appear in the detail pane.

Question 1	How many events appear in the System log?

4. Click Action > Filter Current Log. The Filter Current Log dialog box appears.

5. In the Event Level area, select the Critical check box and the Warning check box. Then click OK.

Question 2	How many events appear in the System log now?

6. Click Actions > Create Custom View. The Create Custom View dialog box appears.

7. In the Logged drop-down list, select Last 7 days.

8. In the Event Level area, select the Critical check box and the Warning check box.

9. Leave the By log option selected and, in the Event logs drop-down list, select the Application, Security, and System check boxes, as shown in Figure 3-1.

Figure 3-1
Selecting the type of logs

10. Click OK. The Save Filter to Custom View dialog box appears.

11. In the Name text box, type Critical & Warning and then click OK. The Critical & Warning view you just created appears in the Custom Views folder.

Question 3	How many events appear in the Critical & Warning custom view?

12. Right-click System (under Windows Logs) and choose Clear Filter.

Leave the Event Viewer console open for the next exercise.

Adding a Task to an Event

1. Using Server Manager, click Tools > Services. The Services console opens.

2. Scroll down and right-click Print Spooler and choose Restart.

3. Go back to Event Viewer. You should have two new entries in the System Logs with an Event ID of 7036. It should read as The Print Spooler service entered the stopped state. Right-click this event and choose Attach Task to This Event.

4. On the Create Basic Task Wizard page, click Next.

5. When the When a Specific Event Is Logged page opens, click Next.

6. On the Action page, make sure Start a program is selected and click Next.

7. On the Start a Program page, type **Notepad** in the Program/script text box. Click Next.

8. On the Summary page, click Finish.

9. Take a screen shot of the Event Viewer dialog box by pressing Alt+Prt Scr and then paste it into your Lab03_worksheetfile in the page provided by pressing Ctrl+V.

10. In the Event Viewer dialog box, click OK.

11. Close Event Viewer.

12. Go back to the Services console. Right-click the Print Spooler service and choose Restart. Notepad should open.

13. Go back to Server Manager. Click Tools >Task Scheduler. Task Scheduler opens.

14. Expand the Task Scheduler Library and click Event Viewer Tasks.

15. Right-click the System_Service Control Manager_7036 task and choose Delete.

16. When you are prompted to confirm that you want to delete this task, click Yes.

17. Close Task Scheduler, the Services console, and Notepad.

Creating a Subscription

1. Log into Server02 as contoso\administrator with the password Pa$$w0rd. The Server Manager console opens.

2. On Server02, right-click Start and choose Command Prompt (Admin).

3. At the command prompt, execute the following command:

```
winrm quickconfig
```

Take Note
It is acceptable that the service is already running.

4. To add the collecting computer name to the Administrators group, execute the following command:

   ```
   net localgroup "Administrators" Server01$@contoso.com/add
   ```

5. If a message appears, indicating that changes must be made, type Y and then press Enter.

6. Go to Server Manager > Tools and click Event Viewer.

7. Click Subscriptions. When you are prompted to confirm that you want to start the Windows Event Collector Service and configure the service to automatically start, click Yes.

8. Close the Command Prompt window.

9. On Server01, unlock the screen by pressing Ctrl+Alt+Delete and entering the password, if needed, then right-click Start and choose Command Prompt (Admin).

10. On Server01, at the command prompt, execute the following command:

    ```
    wecutil qc
    ```

11. If you are prompted to confirm that you want to proceed, type Y and then press Enter.

12. Close the Command Prompt window.

13. Go to Server Manage > Tools menu and open Event Viewer.

14. In Event Viewer, right-click Subscriptions and choose Create Subscription. The Subscription Properties dialog box opens.

15. In the Subscription name text box (as shown in Figure 3-2), type **Server02**.

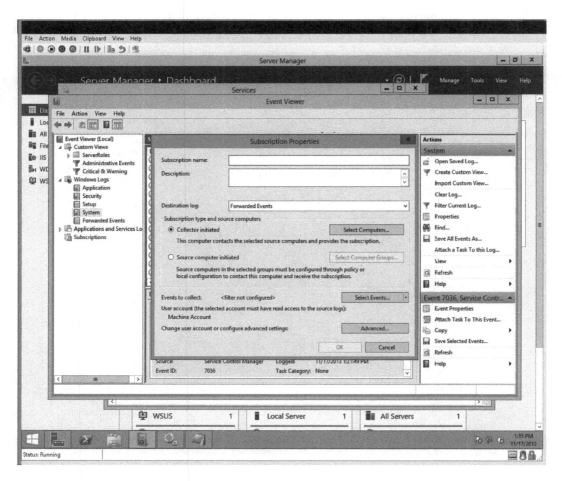

Figure 3-2
Specifying the Subscription Properties

16. Click Select Computers. The Computers dialog box opens.

17. Click Add Domain Computers. In the Enter the object name to select text box, type **Server02** and then click OK.

18. If you are prompted to specify a network password, use the username and password for contoso.com\administrator.

19. Click OK to close Computers dialog box.

20. Click Select Events. The Query Filter dialog box opens.

21. For Event Logs, click System logs.

22. Under Event level, in the Includes/Excludes Event IDs: text box type **7036**, as shown in Figure 3-3. Click **OK** to close Query Filter dialog box.

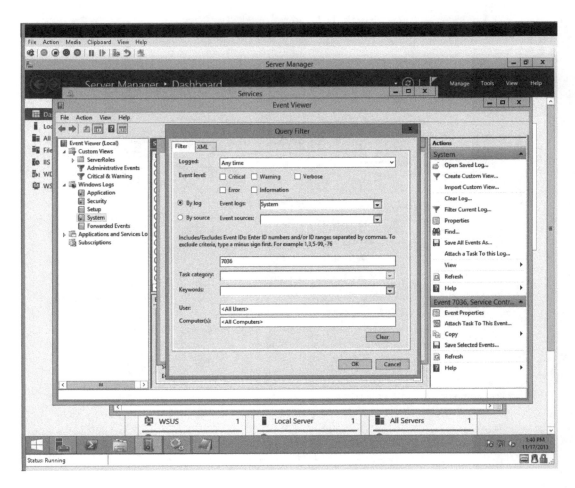

Figure 3-3
Specifying the Event to filter

23. Click OK to close the Subscription Properties dialog box.

24. On Server02, unlock the screen, if needed, then open the Services console from the Tools menu. Right-click Print Spooler and choose Restart. Close the Services console.

25. Go back to Server01. In Event Viewer, under Windows Logs, click Forwarded Events.

Question 4	*Do you see any events? If events do not show, what Windows component could block the packets from being received by the collector computer?*

Question 5	*If you reviewed the configuration of the source computer and the collector computer and you reviewed the firewall, yet you still don't see events, what might cause you not to see the events?*

26. If events do not display immediately, check again later in the lab to see if the events are displayed. If events still fail to appear, disable the Windows firewall on both servers and try again.

27. Take a screen shot of the Event Viewer showing the Forwarded Events by pressing Alt+Prt Scr and then paste it into your Lab03_worksheet file in the page provided by pressing Ctrl+V.

28. Close Event Viewer and the Services console on Server02.

29. Close Event Viewer on Server01.

End of exercise. Close any open windows before you begin the next exercise.

Exercise 3.2	Using Reliability Monitor
Overview	In this exercise, you will use Reliability Monitor to check the status of the computer.
Mindset	The Reliability Monitor is a tool that can determine the reliability of a system, including allowing you to see whether any recent changes have been made to the system itself.
Completion time	15 minutes

1. If you are not logged into Server01, log into Server01 as contoso\administrator with the password Pa$$w0rd. The Server Manager console opens.

2. Click Start, type **regedit,** and then click Enter. The Registry Editor opens.

3. In the left pane, navigate to the HKEY_LOCAL_MACHINE\SOFTWARE\Microsoft\Reliability Analysis\WMI\node.

4. In the right pane, double-click WMIEnable. In the Value data text box, type **1,** as shown in Figure 3-4. Click OK.

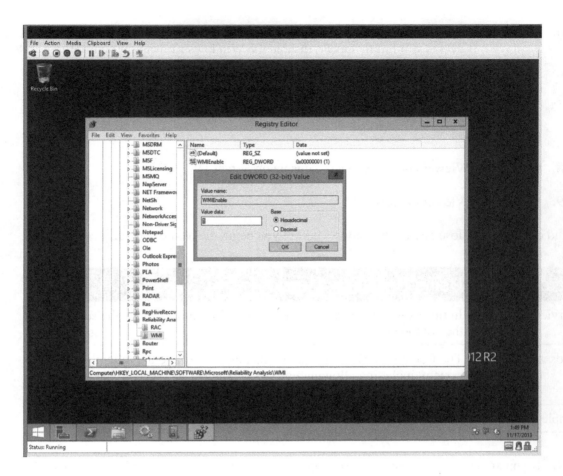

Figure 3-4
Changing the WMIEnable value

5. Close the Registry Editor.

6. In Server Manager, click Tools > Task Scheduler. Task Scheduler opens.

7. In the left pane, navigate to the Task Scheduler > Task Scheduler Library > Microsoft > Windows > RAC.

8. Right-click RacTask and choose Enable.

9. Right-click RacTask and choose Run.

10. Take a screen shot of the Task Scheduler showing the RacTask by pressing Alt+Prt Scr and then paste it into your Lab03_worksheet file in the page provided by pressing Ctrl+V.

11. Close Task Scheduler.

12. Click Start, type **perfmon /rel**, and then click Enter. Reliability Monitor opens.

Question 6	Do you have any events? If you don't have any events, why are the events not displayed?

13. At the bottom of the screen, click View all problem reports.

Question 7	Were there any problems reported?

14. Click OK to close the Problem Reports window.

15. If the reliability reports does not show events with the primary graph, check later to see whether any events are displayed.

16. Click OK to close Reliability Monitor.

End of exercise. Close any open windows before you begin the next exercise.

Exercise 3.3	Using Task Manager
Overview	In this exercise, you will use Task Manager to look at a system and use it to help you manage the system.
Mindset	Task Manager is a simple yet powerful troubleshooting tool you can use to look at overall performance, to view running applications and processes, and to stop applications and processes.
Completion time	15 minutes

1. On Server01, right-click the Task bar and choose Task Manager.

Question 8	What applications are running?

Question 9	What tabs are shown?

2. Click More Details.

Question 10	What tabs are shown?

3.   If Server Manager is not open, open Server Manager.

4.   Open WordPad.

Question 11	In the Apps section, what processes are used for the Server Manager and WordPad?

5.   Click Fewer details.

6.   Right-click Windows Wordpad Application and choose End Task.

7.   Click More details.

8.   Right-click Server Manager and choose Open file location. The System32 folder opens.

9.   Close the System32 folder.

Question 12	How much memory is Server Manager using?

10.   Right-click the Name title at the top of the first column and choose Process name (as shown in Figure 3-5).

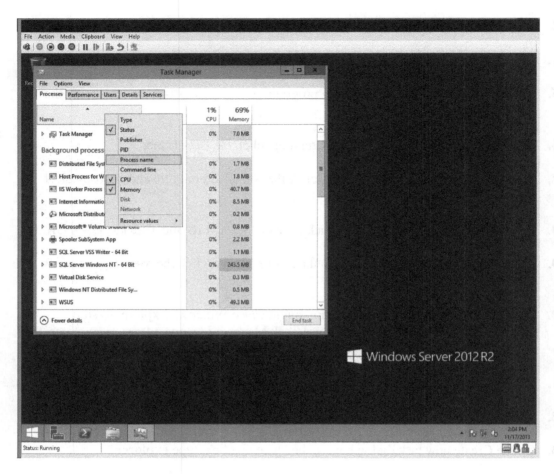

Figure 3-5
Adding the Process name so that it can also be displayed

11. Right-click Server Manager and choose End Task.

12. Click the Performance tab.

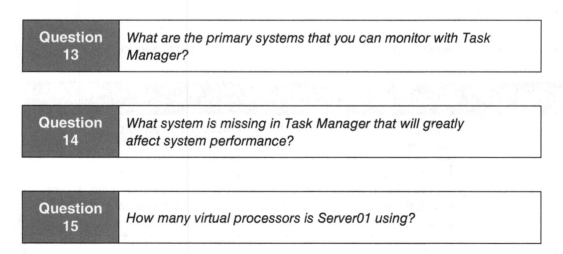

Question 13	What are the primary systems that you can monitor with Task Manager?

Question 14	What system is missing in Task Manager that will greatly affect system performance?

Question 15	How many virtual processors is Server01 using?

13. Click Memory and then click Ethernet to view what each option has to offer.

14. Click the Users tab.

15. Expand Administrator to display the programs and processes being executed by the administrator.

16. To see a detailed list of all processes running, click the Details tab.

17. To display additional columns, right-click the Name column title and choose Select columns.

18. In the Select columns dialog box, click to select Session ID and Threads. Click OK.

19. To sort by components that make up the most memory, click the Memory (private work set) title.

20. From time to time, a program or action might cause Windows Explorer to stop functioning. In these cases, you can use Task Manager to stop and restart Explorer. Find and right-click explorer.exe and then choose End Task.

21. When you are prompted to confirm that you want to end explorer.exe, click End process.

22. Click File >Run new task.

23. On the Create new task dialog box, in the Open text box, type **explorer**.

24. Take a screen shot of the Create new task page by pressing Alt+Prt Scr and then paste it into your Lab03_worksheet file in the page provided by pressing Ctrl+V.

25. Click OK.

26. To view the current services, click the Services tab.

27. Close Task Manager.

End of exercise. Close any open windows before you begin the next exercise.

Exercise 3.4	Using Resource Monitor
Overview	In this exercise, you will use Resource Manager to monitor server resources.
Mindset	The four primary systems in any computer are CPU, memory, disk, and network. A bottleneck can be caused if one of the systems cannot keep up with the current request, which causes the other systems to wait for the lagging system to catch up.
Completion time	5 minutes

1. On Server01, click Start, type **resource monitor**, and then click Enter. The Resource Monitor opens.

Question 16	What are the primary systems that you can monitor with Resource Monitor?

2. Click the CPU tab.

3. To sort the processes alphabetically, click the Image title at the top of the first column in the Processes section.

4. Click the Memory tab.

Question 17	What process is using the most memory?

5. Click the Disk tab.

Question 18	What process is performing the most disk activity?

6. Click the Network tab.

Question 19	What ports are being used by WDSServer?

7. Close Resource Monitor.

End of exercise. Close any open windows before you begin the next exercise.

Exercise 3.5	Using Performance Monitor
Overview	In this exercise, you will open Performance Monitor and view various counters over a period of time.
Mindset	Although Task Manager and Resource Manager gave you a quick look at your system performance, Performance Monitor allows you to thoroughly exam the performance of a system.
Completion time	20 minutes

Using Counters with Performance Monitor

1. On Server01, open Server Manager.

2. Click Tools > Performance Monitor.

3. Browse to and click Monitoring Tools\Performance Monitor.

4. At the bottom of the screen, click % Processor Time. To remove the counter, click the Delete button (the red X) at the top of the Window (the toolbar).

5. On the toolbar, click the Add button (green plus (+) sign) . The Add Counters dialog box appears.

6. Under Available counters, expand Processor, click % Processor Time, and click Show description, as shown in Figure 3-6. Read the description for % Processor Time.

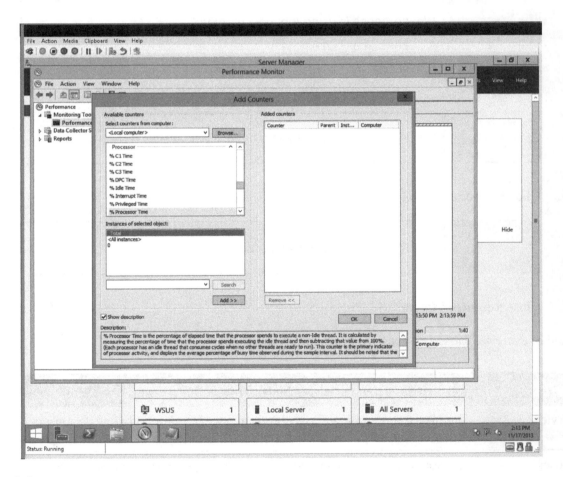

Figure 3-6
Looking at the description of a counter

7. Click Add. % Processor Time should appear in the Added counters section.

8.   Under Available Counters, expand the Server Work Queues and click the Queue Length counter. Under Instances of selected objects, click 0. Then click Add.

9.   Add the following counters:

    - System: Processor Queue Length
    - Memory: Page Faults/Sec
    - Memory: Pages/Sec
    - PhysicalDisk (_Total): Current Disk Queue Length

10.   Click OK to close the Add Counters dialog box.

11.   Open Task Manager and then close Task Manager. You should see a spike in CPU usage.

12.   At the top of the graph, you should see a toolbar with 13 buttons. Click the down arrow of the Change graph type (third button) and then click Histogram bar.

13.   Change the graph type to Report.

14.   Change the graph type back to the Line graph.

15.   On the toolbar, click the Properties button (the fourth button from the right). The Performance Monitor Properties sheet appears. Notice the counters that you have selected.

16.   Click Processor (_Total)\%Processor Time.

17.   Change the width to the heaviest line width. Change the color to Red.

18.   Click the Graph tab.

19.   In the Vertical scale box, change the value of the Maximum field to 200 and then click OK.

Using DCS

1.   In the left pane, expand Data Collector Sets.

2.   Right-click the User Defined folder and choose New > Data Collector Set. In the Name: text box, type **MyDCS1**.

3.   Click Create manually (Advanced) and then click Next.

4.   Select Performance Counter and then click Next.

5.   To add counters, click Add.

6.   Under Available Counters, expand the Processor node by clicking the down arrow next to Processor. Scroll down and click %Processor Time. Click Add.

7. Add the following counters.

- Server Work Queues: Queue Length
- System: Processor Queue Length
- Memory: Page Faults/Sec
- Memory: Pages/Sec
- PhysicalDisk (_Total): Current Disk Queue Length

8. Click OK and then click Next.

9. Click Finish.

10. Right-click MyDCS1 and choose Start.

11. Let it run for at least two minutes.

12. Right-click MyDCS1 and choose Stop.

13. Open Windows Explorer and navigate to c:\PerfLogs\Admin\MyDCS1. Then open the folder that you just created.

14. Double-click DataCollector01.blg. The Performance Monitor graph opens.

Question 20	Now that the DCS has been created, what advantages does the MyDCS1 have?

15. Take a screen shot of the Performance Monitor window by pressing Alt+Prt Scr and then paste it into your Lab03_worksheet file in the page provided by pressing Ctrl+V.

16. Close the Performance Monitor graph and the MyDCS1 folder.

17. Close Performance Monitor.

End of exercise. Close any open windows before you begin the next exercise.

Exercise 3.6	Monitoring VMs
Overview	In this exercise, you will use Windows PowerShell commands to view resource metering.
Mindset	If you have a physical server with multiple virtual machines, you need to ensure that one virtual machine does not consume too much assigned resources.
Completion time	5 minutes

> **NOTE**
>
> *To restart this lab, you must sign off and then sign on again.*

> **NOTE**
>
> *If you do not have access to the hosting server that is running Hyper-V, you will not be able to perform this exercise.*

1. On Student01 (the Hyper-V hosting server), click the Windows PowerShell button on the taskbar.

2. To enable Hyper-V resource metering, execute the followng command, where XX is your student number:

   ```
   Get-VM -ComputerName StudentXX | Enable-VMResourceMetering
   ```

3. By default, the collection interval for Hyper-V metering data is one hour. To change the interval to one minute, execute the following command, again, where XX is your student number:

   ```
   Set-vmhost –computername StudentXX
   -ResourceMeteringSaveInterval 00:01:00
   ```

4. To get all VMs metering data for a host, execute the following command, again, where XX is your student number:

   ```
   Get-VM -ComputerName StudentXX | Measure-VM
   ```

> **Question 21**
>
> *What cmdlet is used to stop VMResourceMetering?*

5. Close Windows PowerShell.

End of exercise.

LAB REVIEW QUESTIONS

Completion time	10 minutes

1. In Exercise 3.1, a busy server over a significant period of time will have hundreds, or even thousands, of events in the Event Viewer logs. When scanning the logs, what must you do in order to find certain relevant events?

2. In Exercise 3.1, what can you use to have one server catch errors from multiple servers that are displayed in Event Viewer?

3. In Exercise 3.2, what program allows you to see a history of recent changes?

4. In Exercise 3.3, what is a powerful tool that allows you to monitor current running programs and processes and allows you to stop those programs and processes?

5. In Exercise 3.4, what program allows you to monitor the four primary systems that affect the overall system performance?

6. In Exercise 3.5, why did you want to create Data Collector Sets?

7. In Exercise 3.6, what did you use to monitor the resources running VMs on Hyper-V?

Lab Challenge	Using Network Monitor
Overview	To complete this challenge, you must demonstrate how to use Network Monitor. The NM32_x64 is located in the \\rwdc01\software folder.
Mindset	You want to look at what steps make a DHCP server work. Therefore, on Server02, you decide to install Microsoft Network Monitor 3.4. You want to capture the packets being sent to and from Server02 and filter the packets to show you only the DNS when using the `nslookup server01` command. The Network Monitor installation program is on the RWDC01 server in C:\Software folder.
Completion time	20 minutes

Write out the steps you performed to complete the challenge.

End of lab.

LAB 4
CONFIGURING DISTRIBUTED FILE SYSTEM (DFS)

THIS LAB CONTAINS THE FOLLOWING EXERCISES AND ACTIVITIES:

Exercise 4.1   Installing DFS

Exercise 4.2   Configuring DFS Namespace

Exercise 4.3   Configuring DFS Replication

Lab Challenge   Creating a Fault-Tolerant Shared Folder

BEFORE YOU BEGIN

The lab environment consists of student workstations connected to a local area network, along with a server that functions as the domain controller for a domain called *contoso.com*. The computers required for this lab are listed in Table 4-1.

Table 4-1
Computers Required for Lab 4

Computer	Operating System	Computer Name
Server (VM 1)	Windows Server 2012 R2	RWDC01
Server (VM 2)	Windows Server 2012 R2	Server01
Server (VM 3)	Windows Server 2012 R2	Server02

In addition to the computers, you also require the software listed in Table 4-2 to complete Lab 4.

Table 4-2
Software Required for Lab 4

Software	Location
Lab 4 student worksheet	Lab04_worksheet.docx (provided by instructor)

Working with Lab Worksheets

Each lab in this manual requires that you answer questions, take screen shots, and perform other activities that you will document in a worksheet named for the lab, such as Lab04_worksheet.docx. You will find these worksheets on the book companion site. It is recommended that you use a USB flash drive to store your worksheets so you can submit them to your instructor for review. As you perform the exercises in each lab, open the appropriate worksheet file using Word, fill in the required information, and save the file to your flash drive.

After completing this lab, you will be able to:

■ Install DFS

■ Implement and configure DFS namespace

■ Implement and configure DFS replication

■ Use DFS for fault tolerant shared folders

Estimated lab time: 80 minutes

Exercise 4.1	Installing DFS
Overview	In this exercise, you will install DFS (namespace and replication) on Server01 and Server02. In Exercise 4.2 and Exercise 4.3, you will configure DFS.
Mindset	Distributed File System improves on the use of the shared folders by enabling you to organize your shared folders and enabling you to distribute shares on multiple servers.
Completion time	10 minutes

1. Log into Server01 as contoso\administrator with the password Pa$$w0rd. The Server Manager console opens.

2. Click Manage > Add Roles and Features. The Add Roles and Feature Wizard opens.

3. On the Before you begin page, click Next.

4. Select Role-based or feature-based installation and then click Next.

5. When you are prompted to select a server, click **Next**.

6. Scroll down and expand File and Storage Services and then expand File and iSCSI Services. Select File Server (if not already installed), DFS Namespaces, and DFS Replication. When you are prompted to add features to DFS Namespace, click Add Features.

Question 1	What does the File Server role do?

7. When you are back on the Select server roles page, click Next.

8. On the Select features page, click Next.

9. On the Confirm installation selections page, click Install.

10. When the installation is complete, take a screen shot of the Add Roles and Features Wizard page by pressing Alt+Prt Scr and then paste it into your Lab04_worksheet file in the page provided by pressing Ctrl+V.

11. Click Close.

12. Repeat the process to install File Server, DFS Namespaces, and DFS replication on Server02.

End of exercise. Close any open windows on Server01 and Server02 before you begin the next exercise.

Exercise 4.2	Configuring DFS Namespace
Overview	In this exercise, you will create several shared folders and then link them together with DFS Namespace.
Mindset	You work for a corporation that has several file servers with multiple shared folders. You want to make it easier for users to access the shared folders. What can you do?
Completion time	25 minutes

1. On Server01, open File Explorer and create folders named **C:\Share1** and **C:\Share2**.

2. Right-click Share1 and choose Properties. The Properties dialog box opens.

3. Click the Sharing tab and then click Advanced Sharing.

4. Select the Share this folder check box.

5. Click Permissions. Click Allow Full Control for Everyone. Click OK to close the Permissions dialog box.

Question 2	Because we allow everyone full control, how do you make sure that the shared files are secure?

6. Click OK to close Advanced Sharing dialog box and click Close to close the Share1 Properties dialog box.

7. On Server01, repeat the process to share Share2.

8. On Server02, unlock the screen, if needed, then open File Explorer and create folders named **C:\Share1** and **C:\Share2**.

9. Similar to what was done on Server01, share the Share1 and Share2 on Server02.

10. On Server01, with Server Manager, click Tools > DFS Management to open the DFS Management console.

11. In the left-pane, right-click Namespaces and choose New Namespace. The New Namespace Wizard starts.

12. On the Namespace Server page, in the Server text box, type **Server01** and then click Next.

13. On the Namespace Name and Settings page, in the Name text box, type **Shares**.

14. Click Edit Settings. The Edit Settings dialog box opens (see Figure 4-1).

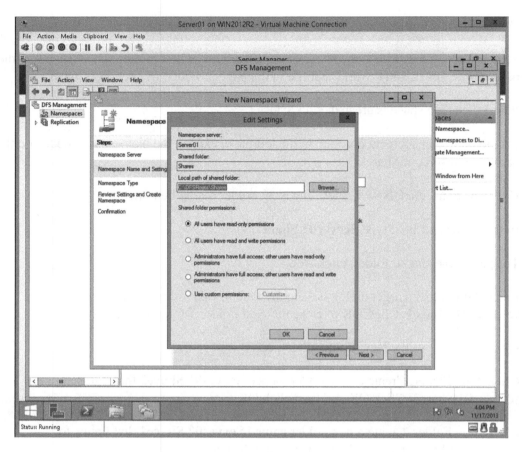

Figure 4-1
Specifying Share permissions for a DFS namespace

Question 3	What is the default location for the shares folder?

15. Click All users have read and write permissions. Click OK to close the Edit Settings dialog box.

16. On the Namespace Name and Settings page, click Next.

Question 4	What is the name of the domain-based namespace?

17. On the Namespace Type page, with Domain-based namespace already selected and Enable Windows Server 2008 mode selected, click Next.

Question 5	What is the advantage of Windows Server 2008 mode?

18. On the Review Settings and Create Namespace page, click Create.

19. Take a screen shot of the New Namespace Wizard page by pressing Alt+Prt Scr and then paste it into your Lab04_worksheet file in the page provided by pressing Ctrl+V.

20. When the name space is created, click **Close**.

21. On the DFS Management console, in the left pane, expand the Namespaces node and then click \\contoso.com\Shares.

22. Under Actions, click New Folder. The New Folder dialog box opens.

23. In the Name text box, type **Server01 Share1**.

24. To specify the shared folder, click Add.

25. In the Add Folder Target dialog box, in the Path to folder target text box, type **\\Server01\Share1**. Click OK to close the Add Folder Target dialog box.

26. Click OK to close the New Folder dialog box.

27. Click New Folder. Create a new folder named **Server01 Share2** that points to \\Server01\Share2. Click OK and then click OK again.

28. Click New Folder. Create a new folder named **Server02 Share1** that points to \\Server02\Share1. Click OK and then click OK again.

29. Click New Folder. Create a new folder named **Server02 Share2** that points to \\Server02\Share2. Click OK and then click OK again.

30. On Server01, open File Explorer. In the Location text box, type **\\contoso.com\shares** and then press Enter.

31. Take a screen shot of the Shares folder by pressing Alt+Prt Scr and then paste it into your Lab04_worksheet file in the page provided by pressing Ctrl+V.

32. Close File Explorer.

33. On the DFS Management console, right-click the \\Contoso.com\Shares namespace and choose Properties. The Properties dialog box opens.

34. Click the Advanced tab.

35. Select the Enable access-based enumeration for this namespace checkbox.

36. Take a screen shot of the \\contoso.com\Shares Properties dialog box by pressing Alt+Prt Scr and then paste it into your Lab04_worksheet file in the page provided by pressing Ctrl+V.

Question 6	*What does the* Enable access-based enumeration for this namespace *option do?*

37. Click OK to close the Properties dialog box.

End of exercise. Close any open windows before you begin the next exercise.

Exercise 4.3	Configuring DFS Replication
Overview	In this exercise, you will configure two folders, each on a different server. You will then configure DFS to replicate the content of one folder to the other server.
Mindset	You have a project folder that must be available in New York and Paris. Some of these files are large, so they take some time to open over a slow WAN link. You can use DFS Replication to create a replicate of the file share at both offices.
Completion time	30 minutes

1. On Server01, create a folder named **C:\Share3**. Share the folder as Share3. Assign Allow Full Control Share permissions to Everyone.

2. On Server02, unlock the screen, if needed, then create a folder named **C:\Share3**. Share the folder as Share3. Assign Allow Full Control Share permissions to Everyone.

3. On Server01, in the DFS Management console, right-click Replication and choose New Replication Group.

4. On the Replication Group Type page, click Next.

5. On the Name and Domain page, in the Name of replication group text box, type **Rep1** and then click Next.

6. On the Replication Group Members page, click Add.

7. In the Select Computers dialog box, in the Enter the object names to select text box, type **Server01** and then click OK. If you are prompted to enter a network password, use contoso\administrator and a password of Pa$$w0rd.

8. Click Add and then add Server02.

9. Take a screen shot of the New Replication Group Wizard page by pressing Alt+Prt Scr and then paste it into your Lab04_worksheet file in the page provided by pressing Ctrl+V.

10. Back on the Replication Group Members page, click Next.

11. On the Topology Selection page, click Next.

12. On the Replication Group Schedule and Bandwidth page, click Next.

Question 7	*If you have limited available bandwidth between two sites, what can you do to make better use of the available bandwidth so that users are not hampered when accessing remote resources?*

13. On the Primary Member page, select Server01 as the Primary member and then click Next.

14. On the Folders to Replicate page, click Add.

15. In the Add Folder to Replicate dialog box, in the Local path of folder to replicate text box, type **C:\Share3** and then click OK.

16. Back on the Folders to Replicate page (see Figure 4-2), click Next.

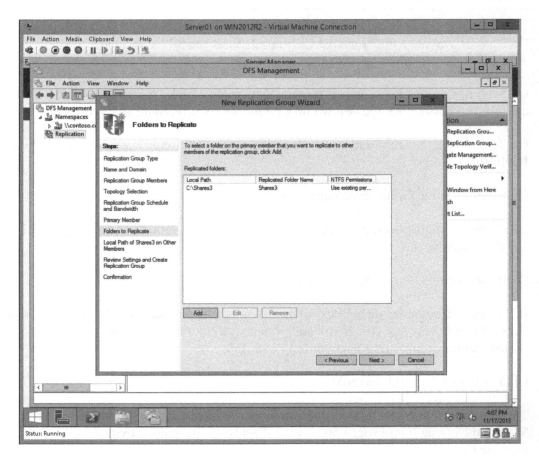

Figure 4-2
Adding folders to replicate

17. On the Local Path of Share3 on Other Members page, with Server02 selected, click Edit.

18. Click Enabled and in the Local path of folder text box, type **C:\Share3**. Click OK to close the Edit dialog box.

19. Back on the Local Path of Share3 on Other Members page, click Next.

20. On the Review Settings and Create Replication Group page, click Create.

21. When the replication group has been created, click Close.

22. If a Replication Delay message is displayed, click OK.

23. Expand the Replication node, and click the Repl node.

24. Take a screen shot of the DFS Management console by pressing Alt+Prt Scr and then paste it into your Lab04_worksheet worksheet file in the page provided by pressing Ctrl+V.

25. On Server01, open the C:\Share3 folder with File Explorer.

26. Right-click the opened folder and choose New > Text Document. Name the document **Doc1.txt**.

27. Open the Doc1.txt file and type your name. Save and then close the document.

28. On Server02, open the C:\Share3 folder and verify that the Doc1 text file has replicated to Server02. It may take a minute or two to replicate.

29. Under the Membership tab, right-click the SERVER01 Share3, and click Properties.

30. When the SERVER01 (Share3) Properties dialog box opens, click the Staging tab.

Question 8	*What is the default quota for the staging path?*

31. Change the quota to 8192 MB.

32. Click the Advanced tab.

Question 9	*What is the default quota for Conflict and Deleted path?*

33. Click OK to close the SERVER01 (Share3) Properties dialog box.

34. Right-click the SERVER02 Share3, and click Properties.

35. Click the Staging tab.

36. Change the Quota to 8192 MB.

37. Click OK to close the SERVER02 (Share3) Properties dialog box.

38. Take a screen shot of the *DFS Management* console by pressing Alt+Prt Scr and then paste it into your Lab04_worksheet worksheet file in the page provided by pressing Ctrl+V.

End of exercise. Close any windows that are open on Server01 and Server02.

LAB REVIEW QUESTIONS

Completion time	5 minutes

1. In Exercise 4.2, what technology was used to create a shared folder of shared folders?

2. In Exercise 4.2, where is the configuration for domain-based namespaces stored?

3. In Exercise 4.3, what technology is used to automatically copy files from one server to another?

4. In Exercise 4.3, what topology is used to have files replicate from one member to all other DFS members?

Lab Challenge	Creating a Fault-Tolerant Shared Folder
Overview	To complete this challenge, you will create a high-level list that describes how to create a fault-tolerant shared folder.
Mindset	You have content that is contained in a folder that you want to make available, even if a file server becomes unavailable. What do you need to do in order to accomplish this?
Completion time	10 minutes

Write out the steps you performed to complete the challenge.

End of lab.

LAB 5
CONFIGURING FILE SERVER RESOURCE MANAGER

THIS LAB CONTAINS THE FOLLOWING EXERCISES AND ACTIVITIES:

Exercise 5.1   Installing File Server Resource Manager

Exercise 5.2   Configuring Quotas

Exercise 5.3   Managing Files with File Screening

Exercise 5.4   Using Storage Reports

Exercise 5.5   Configuring File Management Tasks

Lab Challenge   Enabling SMTP for FSRM

BEFORE YOU BEGIN

The lab environment consists of student workstations connected to a local area network, along with a server that functions as the domain controller for a domain called *contoso.com*. The computers required for this lab are listed in Table 5-1.

Table 5-1
Computers Required for Lab 5

Computer	Operating System	Computer Name
Server (VM 1)	Windows Server 2012 R2	RWDC01
Server (VM 2)	Windows Server 2012 R2	Server01

In addition to the computers, you also require the software listed in Table 5-2 to complete Lab 5.

Table 5-2
Software Required for Lab 5

Software	Location
ADMXMigrator.msi, NMI32_x64.exe, System Center Monitoring Pack for File and Storage Management.msi, and Windows8.1-KB2901549.msu	C:\Software
Lab 5 student worksheet	Lab05_worksheet.docx (provided by instructor)

Working with Lab Worksheets

Each lab in this manual requires that you answer questions, take screen shots, and perform other activities that you will document in a worksheet named for the lab, such as Lab05_worksheet.docx. You will find these worksheets on the book companion site. It is recommended that you use a USB flash drive to store your worksheets, so you can submit them to your instructor for review. As you perform the exercises in each lab, open the appropriate worksheet file using Word, fill in the required information, and save the file to your flash drive.

After completing this lab, you will be able to:

- Install and configure File Server Resource Manager

- Use Quotas to manage disk space

- Manage files with file screening

- Use Storage Reports

Estimated lab time: 90 minutes

Exercise 5.1	Installing File Server Resource Manager
Overview	During this exercise, you install File Server Resource Manager (FSRM), which is used in the following exercises.
Mindset	The File Server Resource Manager is a suite of tools that enables you to control and manage the quantity and type of data stored on a file server. It enables you to define how much data a person can store, define what type of files a user can store on a file server, and generate reports about the file server being used.
Completion time	10 minutes

1. Log in to Server01 using the Contoso\Administrator account and the password Pa$$w0rd.

2. On Server01, at the top of Server Manager, select Manage and click Add Roles and Features to open the Add Roles and Feature Wizard.

3. On the Before you begin page, click Next.

4. Select Role-based or feature-based installation and then click Next.

5. When it asks for your destination server, click Next.

6. Scroll down, expand File and Storage Services, and expand File and iSCSI Services. Select File Server Resource Manager.

7. When you are asked to add additional features, click Add Features.

8. On the Select server roles page, click Next.

9. On the Select features page, click Next.

10. On the Confirm installation selections page, click Install.

11. When the installation is complete, take a screen shot of the File Server Resource Manager installation by pressing Alt+Prt Scr and then paste it into your Lab05_worksheet file in the page provided by pressing Ctrl+V.

12. Click Close.

End of exercise. You can leave the windows open for the next exercise.

Exercise 5.2	Configuring Quotas
Overview	During this exercise, you use File Server Resource Manager quotas.
Mindset:	When you configure quotas for NTFS, you configure quotas based on user files stored on a volume. FSRM specifies the total space for a volume or folder.
Completion time	10 minutes

1. On Server01, using File Explorer, create a Share4 folder in the C:\ folder.

2. Share the Share4 folder and specify Allow Full Control for Everyone.

3. In Server Manager, click Tools > File Server Resource Manager. The File Server Resource Manager console opens.

4. Expand Quota Management and then click Quota Templates. Then right-click Quota Templates and select Create Quota Template. The Create Quota Template dialog box opens.

5. In the Template name text box, type QuotaTemplate1.

6. In the Space limit section, in the Limit text box, type **10** and then specify the unit MB.

7. Select Soft quota, as shown in Figure 5-1.

Question 1	What is the difference between a hard and soft quota?

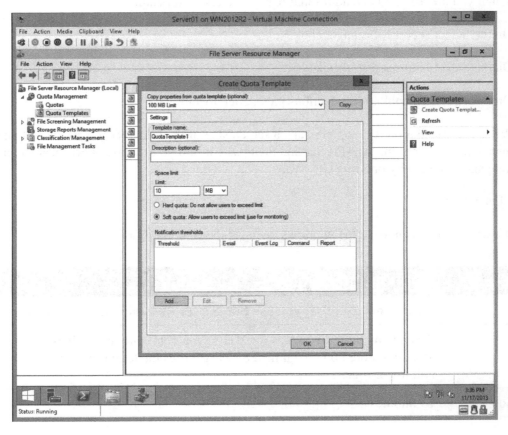

Figure 5-1
Creating a quota template

8. To add a notification, click the Add button. The Add Threshold dialog box opens.

9. Click the Event Log tab.

10. Select the Send warning to event log check box.

11. Click OK to save your notification threshold and close the Add Threshold dialog box.

12. Click OK to close the Create Quota Template dialog box.

13. Click the Quota Templates node and take a screen shot of the Quota Templates pane by pressing Alt+Prt Scr and then paste it into your Lab05_worksheet file in the page provided by pressing Ctrl+V.

14. Under the Quota Management node, click the Quota Templates node.

15. Right-click the QuotaTemplate1 in the Quota Templates pane and click the Create Quota from Template option. The Create Quota dialog box opens.

16. In the Quota path, type **c:\Share4** in the Quota path text box.

17. Click Create.

18. Open File Manager, navigate to the \\RWDC01\software folder, and then copy the following files to the C:\Share4 folder:

- ADMXMigrator.msi
- NM34_x64.exe
- System Center Monitoring Pack for File and Storage Management.msi
- Windows8.1-KB2901549-x64.msu

19. On Server01, open the Event Viewer and look for an entry in the Application logs showing that the quota has been exceeded.

Question 2	What event ID was used for the quota to be exceeded?

20. Take a screen shot of the Event Viewer window by pressing Alt+Prt Scr and then paste it into your Lab05_worksheet file in the page provided by pressing Ctrl+V.

21. Close Event Viewer.

End of exercise. You can leave the windows open for the next exercise.

Exercise 5.3	Managing Files with File Screening
Overview	During this exercise, you continue to use File Server Resource Manager by using File Screening.
Mindset	You have a file server that ran out of disk space. Last week, there was plenty of space and this week, there is none. While looking at the files that are stored, you noticed that a couple of users have stored movie and music collections. File Screening allows you to prevent certain files from being saved to a folder based on the filename extension.
Completion time	20 minutes

1. On Server01, on File Server Resource Manager, expand File Screening Management.

2. Click the File Groups node.

3. Right-click File Groups and select Create File Group. The Create File Group Properties dialog box opens.

4. In the File group name text box, type **FileGroup1**.

5. To include video files and add all files with the filename extension ram, type ***.ram**, and then click Add.

6. Add the following filename extensions:

   *.rm

   *.avi

   *.wmv

   *.mpg

7. To add files to exclude, type **hello.avi** in the Files to exclude text box and click Add. The Create File Group Properties dialog box should look like Figure 5-2.

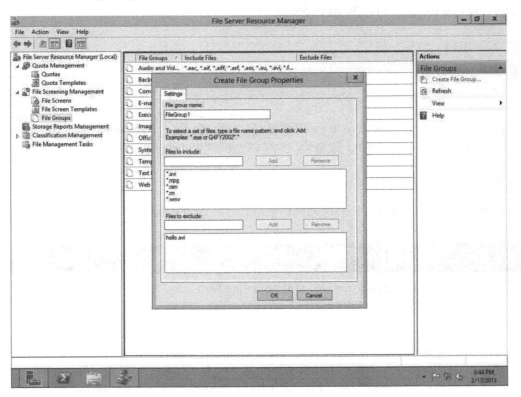

Figure 5-2
Creating file groups

8. Click OK to close the Create File Group Properties dialog box.

9. Under File Screening Management, click the File Screens node.

10. Right-click File Screens, and then click Create File Screen. The Create File Screen dialog box opens.

11. Type **C:\Share4** in the File screen path text box.

12. Click Define custom file screen properties and then click Custom Properties. The File Screen Properties dialog box opens.

13. With Active screening already selected, select FileGroup1 in the File groups section.

14. To log an event, click the Event Log tab. Then click to select the Send warning to event log check box.

15. Click OK to close the File Screen Properties dialog box.

16. Click Create to create a new file screen.

17. When you are prompted to save the custom properties as a template, click Save the custom file screen without creating a template. Click OK.

18. With File Explorer, open the C:\Share4 folder.

19. In File Explorer, click the View tab.

20. Ensure that File name extensions is selected as shown in Figure 5-3.

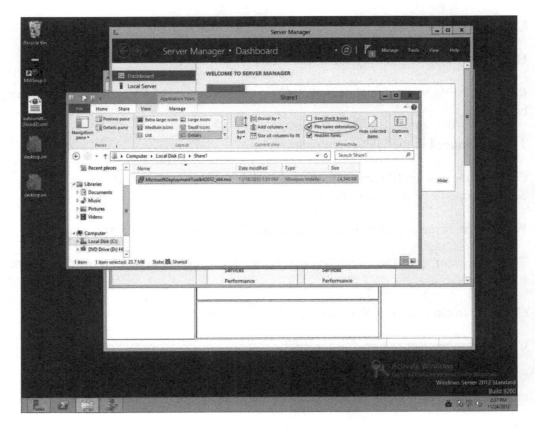

Figure 5-3
Showing File name extensions

21. On the Desktop, create a text file named **test1.avi**. Be sure that the file does not have the .txt filename extension. If it asks to change the filename extension, click OK.

> **NOTE** *Although the file has a .avi filename extension, it is really not a video file. It is just to demonstrate file screening.*

22. Copy the test1.avi file to the C:\Share4 folder.

> **Question 3** *What message did you get when you tried to copy the file?*

23. Click Cancel.

24. Rename the test1.avi file to **hello.avi**.

25. Copy the hello.avi file to the C:\Share4 folder.

26. Open the Event Viewer and access the Application logs.

Question 4	*What event ID was used for files that were not permitted for file screening?*

27. Close Event Viewer.

28. Close the Share4 folder.

End of exercise. You can leave the windows open for the next exercise.

Exercise 5.4	Using Storage Reports
Overview	During this exercise, you execute File Server Resource Manager storage reports.
Mindset	To help you manage storage, you can use FSRM to generate storage reports that show the state of file server volumes and anyone who exceeds the quota or uses files that aren't allowed.
Completion time	10 minutes

1. On Server01, on File Server Resource Manager, click Storage Reports Management.

2. Right-click Storage Reports Management and click Generate Reports Now.

3. When the Storage Reports Task Properties dialog box opens, in the Report data section, select Quota Usage.

Question 5	*You are starting to run out of space on a volume. Which FSRM report would you use to to determine which files can be archived?*

4. Click the Scope tab.

5. Click Add. Then browse to the C:\Share4 and click OK to close the Browse For Folder dialog box.

6. Click OK to close the Storage Reports Task Properties dialog box.

7. When the Generate Storage Reports dialog box opens, click OK.

8. When a folder opens, double-click the html file. Close message box, if needed, and view the Quota Usage Report.

9. Take a screen shot of the Quota Usage Report window by pressing Alt+Prt Scr and then paste it into your Lab05_worksheet file in the page provided by pressing Ctrl+V.

10. Close Internet Explorer.

Exercise 5.5	Configuring File Management Tasks
Overview	During this exercise, you will create a file management tasks that will expire a files in a data folder.
Mindset	By using the File Management Tasks node in FSRM, you can create file management tasks to handle expiring files. These tasks can automatically move all files that match specified criteria to a specified expiration directory. An administrator can then back those files up and delete them.
Completion time	20 minutes

1. On Server01, using File Explorer, on the C drive, create a C:\FileData folder.

2. In the FileData folder, create a Test1 file with NotePad. Type your name in the text file and save the file.

3. Using File Explorer, create a C:\Expire folder.

4. On File Server Resource Manager, click the File Management Tasks node.

5. Right-click the File Management Tasks node and choose Create File Management Task.

6. When the Create File Management Task dialog box opens, on the General tab, in the Task name text box, type Cleanup Old Files.

7. Click the Scope tab and click the Add button.

8. When the Browse For Folder dialog box opens, navigate to and select the C:\FileData folder. Click OK.

9. Click the Action tab.

10. On the Action tab, File Expiration is selected.

11. Click the Browse button.

12. When the Browse For Folder dialog box opens, navigate to and select the C:\Expire folder.Click OK.

13. Click the Condition tab.

14. Select the Days since file was created. Ensure that 0 days is specified.

15. On the Schedule tab, Specify the task to run on Sundays at 8 pm. Click OK.

16. Right-click the File Management task that you just created, and click Run File Management Tasks Now. Within a minute, the text file should move from the C:\FileData folder to the C:\Expire folder.

17. Take a screen shot of the File Server Resource Manager by pressing Alt+Prt Scr and then paste it into your Lab05_worksheet file in the page provided by pressing Ctrl+V.

18. Close File Server Resource Manager.

LAB REVIEW QUESTIONS

Completion time	10 minutes

1. In Exercise 5.2, with File Server Resource Manager, what are quotas assigned to?

2. In Exercise 5.2, if you want to prevent a folder from getting too large, what type of quota should you use?

3. In Exercise 5.2, what methods can you use for notification when a quota is exceeded?

4. In Exercise 5.3, how do you prevent a user from saving unauthorized files?

5. In Exercise 5.5, what allows you to get a comprehensive report on how a disk is being used by the users?

Lab Challenge	Enabling SMTP for FSRM
Overview	To complete this challenge, you must demonstrate how to enable SMTP for FSRM by writing the steps to complete the tasks described in the scenerio.
Mindset	You just configured quotas and file screening properly. You now want to be e-mailed when quotas are exceeded and when users save unauthorized files. However, the messages are not being forwarded to the e-mail server. What should you do?
Completion time	10 minutes

Write out the steps you performed to complete the challenge.

End of lab.

LAB 6
CONFIGURING FILE SERVICES AND DISK ENCRYPTION

THIS LAB CONTAINS THE FOLLOWING EXERCISES AND ACTIVITIES:

Exercise 6.1   Encrypting Files with EFS

Exercise 6.2   Configuring the EFS Recovery Agent

Exercise 6.3   Backing Up and Restoring EFS Certificates

Exercise 6.4   Encrypting a Volume with BitLocker

Lab Challenge   Deploying Network Unlock

BEFORE YOU BEGIN

The lab environment consists of student workstations connected to a local area network, along with a server that functions as the domain controller for a domain called *contoso.com*. The computers required for this lab are listed in Table 6-1.

Table 6-1
Computers Required for Lab 6

Computer	Operating System	Computer Name
Server (VM 1)	Windows Server 2012 R2	RWDC01
Server (VM 2)	Windows Server 2012 R2	Server01

In addition to the computers, you also require the software listed in Table 6-2 to complete Lab 6.

Table 6-2
Software Required for Lab 6

Software	Location
Lab 6 student worksheet	Lab06_worksheet.docx (provided by instructor)

Working with Lab Worksheets

Each lab in this manual requires that you answer questions, take screen shots, and perform other activities that you will document in a worksheet named for the lab, such as Lab06_worksheet.docx. You will find these worksheets on the book companion site. It is recommended that you use a USB flash drive to store your worksheets, so you can submit them to your instructor for review. As you perform the exercises in each lab, open the appropriate worksheet file using Word, fill in the required information, and save the file to your flash drive.

After completing this lab, you will be able to:

■ Encrypt files with EFS

■ Configure EFS Recovery Agent

■ Back up and restore EFS certificates

■ Encrypt a volume with BitLocker

Estimated lab time: 70 minutes

Exercise 6.1	Encrypting Files with EFS
Overview	For files that are extremely sensitive, you can use EFS to encrypt the files.During this exercise, you encrypt a file using Encrypting File System (EFS), which is a built-in feature of NTFS.
Mindset	Encryption is a way to add an additional layer of security. If the laptop is stolen and the hard drive is put into another system where the thief or hacker is an administrator, the files could not be read without the proper key. If you want to encrypt individual documents, you can use Encrypting File System (EFS).
Completion time	20 minutes

Encrypting Files with EFS

1. Log in to Server01 as the Contoso\administrator user account with the password Pa$$w0rd. The Server Manager console opens.

2. On Server01, create a **C:\Data** folder.

3. Create a text file in the C:\Data folder called **test.txt** file. Open the text file, type your name in the file, close the file, then click Save to save the changes.

4. Right-click the C:\Data folder and choose Properties. The Properties dialog box opens.

5. On the General tab, click Advanced. The Advanced Attributes dialog box appears as shown in Figure 6-1.

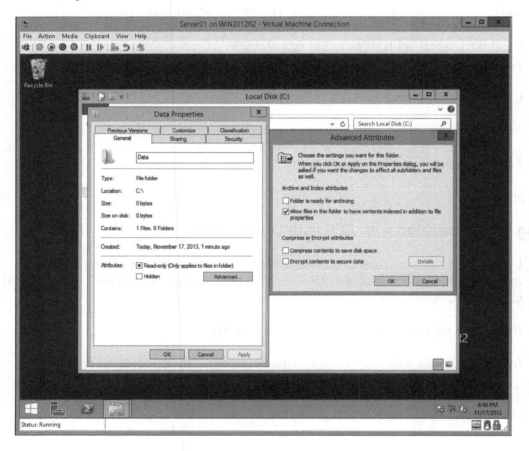

Figure 6-1
Configuring advanced attributes

6. Click to select Encrypt contents to secure data. Click OK to close the Advanced Attributes dialog box.

7. Click OK to close the Properties dialog box.

8. When Windows asks you to confirm the changes, click OK.

Question 1	*What color is the C:\Data folder?*

Question 2	*Is the test.txt file in the C:\Data folder also encrypted?*

9. Right-click the C:\Data folder and choose Properties. The Properties dialog box opens.

10. Under the General tab, click Advanced. The Advanced Attributes dialog box opens.

11. Clear the Encrypt contents to secure data check box. Click OK to close the Advanced Attributes dialog box.

12. Click OK to close the Properties dialog box.

13. When it asks to confirm attribute changes, click OK.

14. From Server01, log off as administrator.

End of exercise.

Sharing Files Protected with EFS with Other Users

1. Log into RWDC01 as contoso\administrator, Server Manager starts. Open the Tools menu and click Active Directory Users and Computers. The Active Directory Users and Computers console opens.

2. Right-click the Users node, click New, then click User.

3. Create a new user with the following parameters:

   First Name: **User1**
   User logon name: **User1**

   Click Next.

4. For the Password and Confirm password text boxes, type **Pa$$w0rd**. Click to select Password never expires. When an Active Directory Domain Services dialog box appears, click OK. Click Next.

5. When the user is ready to be created, click Finish.

6. Under the Users node, double-click User1. The User1 Properties dialog box opens.

7. Click the Member Of tab.

8. Click the Add button. When the Select Groups dialog box opens, type **domain admins** and click OK.

9. Click OK to close the User1 Properties dialog box.

10. On Server01, log in as contoso\User1 with the password of Pa$$w0rd.

11. Open the C:\Data folder, right-click the test.txt file and choose Properties.

12. On the General tab, click Advanced. The Advanced Attributes dialog box opens.

13. Click Encrypt contents to secure data. Click OK to close the Advanced Attributes dialog box. Click OK to close the Properties dialog box.

14. When it asks if you want to encrypt the file and its parent folder, click OK.

15. If an Access Denied message appears, click Ignore, click Continue, click OK, and click Ignore. Click OK. If an Access Denied message appears again, click Ignore All. When you are done, the test.txt file should be green.

16. On Server01, log out as User1 and log in as Contoso\Administrator.

17. Open the C:\Data folder.

18. Double-click to open the Test.txt file.

Question 3	What error message did you get?

19. Click OK to close the message, and then close Notepad.

20. Right-click the test.txt file and click Properties.

21. Click the Security tab.

Question 4	What permissions does Administrator have?

Question 5	Why was the contoso\administrator not able to open the file?

22. Go back to the General tab, click the Advanced button, clear the Encrypt check box, and then click OK.

Question 6	Were you able to decrypt the file?

23. Click OK to close the Properties dialog box. After getting the Access Denied box, click Cancel to close it.

24. On Server01, log off as Administrator and log on as User1.

25. Open the C:\Data folder.

26. Right-click the test.txt file and choose Properties. The Properties dialog box opens.

27. Click the Advanced button to open the Advanced Attributes dialog box.

28. Click to deselect the Encrypt contents to secure data check box and then click OK.

29. Click OK to close the Properties dialog box. When it asks you to provide administrator permission to change these attributes, click Continue.

30. Log off as User1 and log on as contoso\administrator.

31. Open the C:\Data folder.

32. Right-click the Test.txt file and choose Properties.

33. Click the Advanced button to open the Advanced Attributes dialog box.

34. Click to select the Encrypt contents to secure data check box. Click OK to close the Advanced Attributes dialog box.

35. Click OK to close the Properties dialog box. When it asks to apply to the folder and its contents, click OK.

36. Right-click the test.txt file and choose Properties. Click the Advanced button to open the Advanced Attributes dialog box.

37. Click the Details button. The User Access to test.txt dialog box opens.

38. Click the Add button. When the Encrypting File System dialog box opens, click User1 and click View Certificate.

39. When the Certificate dialog box opens, click the Details tab.

Question 7	What is the Certificate used for? Hint: Look at the Enhanced Key Usage field.

40. Click OK to close the Certificates dialog box.

41. Click OK to close the Encrypting File System dialog box.

Question 8	Looking at the User Access to test.txt dialog box, who has a Recovery Certificate?

42. Take a screen shot of the User Access to test dialog box by pressing Alt+Prt Scr and then paste it into your Lab06_worksheet file in the page provided by pressing Ctrl+V.

43. Click OK to close the User Access to test.txt dialog box, click OK to close Advanced Attributes dialog box, and then click OK to close test Properties box.

44. On Server01, sign out as Administrator and log in as User1.

45. Open the C:\Data folder and open the test.txt file.

Question 9	Were you able to open the file?

46. Close the test.txt file.

47. On Server01, sign out as User1.

End of exercise.

Exercise 6.2	Configuring the EFS Recovery Agent
Overview	During this exercise, you configure EFS Recovery Agents so that you can recover EFS encrypted files although the agent is not the owner of the file.
Mindset	When an employee leaves the company, that employee's files might be encrypted, which would be unreadable to anyone else. Using an EFS recovery agent, you will be able to recover those files and make them available to the user or users who have replaced the departed user.
Completion time	15 minutes

Installing and Configuring the Certificate Authority

1. On RWDC01, log on as contoso\administrator, if needed.

2. On RWDC01, on the Server Manager, click Manage > Add Roles and Features.

3. When the Add Roles and Features Wizard starts, click Next.

4. On the Select installation type page, click Next.

5. On the Select destination server page, click Next.

6. On the Select server roles page, click Active Directory Certificate Services. When you are prompted to add features, click Add Features. Then when you are back to the Select server roles page, click Next.

7. On the Select features page, click Next.

8. On the Active Directory Certificate Services page, click Next.

9. On the Select role services, Certification Authority is already selected. Click to select the following:

   Certificate Enrollment Policy Web Service
   Certificate Enrollment Web Service
   Certification Authority Web Enrollment

   When it asks you to add additional features for any of these features, click Add Features.

10. Back on the Select role services page, click Next.

11. On the Web Server Role (IIS) page, click Next.

12. On the Select role services page, click Next.

13. On the Confirm installation selections page, click Install.

14. When the Certificate Authority is installed, click Close.

15. On Server Manager, click the Exclamation Point in a yellow triangle and then click the Configure Active Directory Certificate Services link.

16. On the Credentials page, click Next.

17. On the Role Services page, click Certification Authority, as shown in Figure 6-2. Click Next.

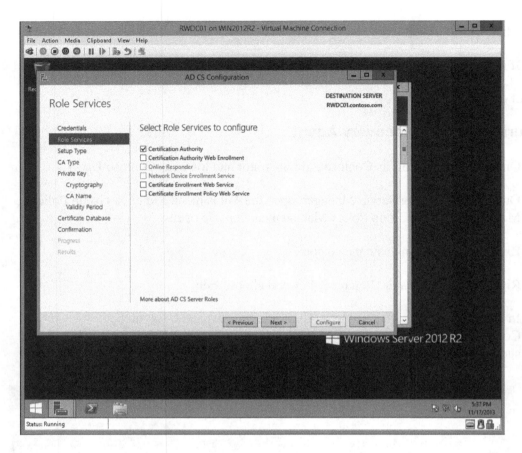

Figure 6-2
Configuring the Certification Authority

18. When it asks what setup type of CA you should install, click Next.

19. When it asks for the CA type, click Next.

20. On the Specify the type of the private key page, click Next.

21. On the Specify the Cryptography for CA page, click Next.

22. On the Specify the name of the CA page, click Next.

23. Change the Validity Period to 10 years and then click Next.

24. On the CA database page, click Next.

25. On the Confirmation page, click Configure.

26. When the CA is configured, take a screen shot of the CA is configured screen by pressing Alt+Prt Scr and then paste it into your Lab06_worksheet file in the page provided by pressing Ctrl+V.

27. Click Close.

28. If it asks to configure additional role services, click No.

End of exercise.

Configuring the EFS Recovery Agent

1. On RWDC01, log off as Contoso\Administrator and log in as Contoso\User1.

2. On RWDC01, using Server Manager, open the **Tools** menu and click Group Policy Management. The Group Policy Management console opens.

3. Expand Forest\Domains\contoso.com.

4. Right-click the Default Domain Policy and choose Edit.

5. In the Group Policy Management Editor window, expand Computer Configuration\Policies\Windows Settings\Security Settings\Public Key Policies\ as shown in Figure 6-3.

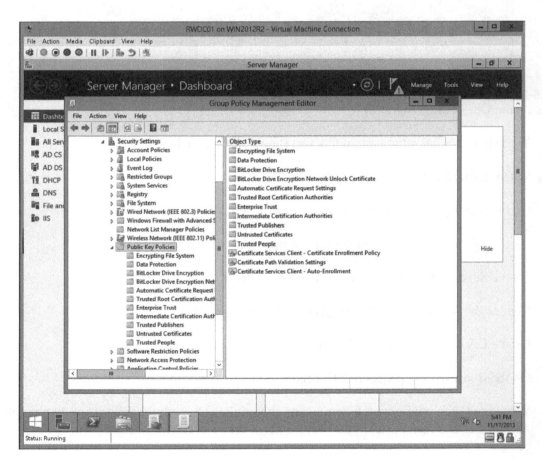

Figure 6-3
Opening the GPO public key policies

6. Right-click Encrypting File System and choose Create Data Recovery Agent.

7. Click the Encrypting File System node. Take a screen shot of the Group Policy Management Editor by pressing Alt+Prt Scr and then paste it into your Lab06_worksheet file in the page providedby pressing Ctrl+V.

8. On RWDC01, log off as Contoso\User1 and log in as Contoso\Administrator.

Question 10	What is needed for a user to become a data recovery agent?

End of exercise. You can leave the windows open for the next exercise.

Exercise 6.3   Backing Up and Restoring EFS Certificates

Overview	During this exercise, you back up an EFS certificate which you later restore after you delete the certificate.
Mindset	You have a standalone computer that failed and had to be rebuilt. On the computer, you had some files that were encrypted with EFS. Fortunately, you backed up the files from time to time to a removable drive. After you rebuilt the computer, you copied the files from the removable drive. Although you are using the same username and password that you used before, you cannot open the files because they are encrypted. Unfortunately, there is not much you can do unless you have the EFS certificates with the correct keys to decipher the documents. Therefore, it is important that you always have a back up of the EFS certificates in case the system needs to be replaced.
Completion time	10 minutes

Backing Up the EFS Certificates

1. Log on to Server01 as contoso\administrator. The Server Manager console opens.

2. Right-click the Start button and choose Command Prompt (Admin).

3. From the command prompt, execute the `certmgr.msc` command. The certmgr console opens.

4. In the left pane, double-click Personal, and then click Certificates.

5. In the main pane, right-click the certificate that lists Encrypting File System under Intended Purposes. Select All Tasks, and then click Export.

6. When the Certificate Export Wizard starts, click Next.

7. On the Export Private Key page, click Yes, export the private key and then click Next.

8. On the Export File Format page, click Next.

9. On the Security page, select the Password check box and type the password of **Pa$$w0rd** in the Password and Confirm password text boxes. Click Next.

Question 11	*What is the difference between the cer and the pfx format when backing up digital certificates?*

10. On the File to Export page, type **C:\Cert.bak** in the File name text box, Click Next.

11. Take a screen shot of the Completing the Certificate Export Wizard by pressing Alt+Prt Scr and then paste it into your Lab08_worksheet file in the page provided by pressing Ctrl+V.

12. When the wizard is complete, click Finish.

13. When the export is successful, click OK.

Restoring the EFS Certificate

1. Right-click the Administrator certificate and click Delete. When it asks if you want to delete the certificate, read the warning and click Yes.

2. Right-click Certificates and choose All Tasks > Import.

3. When the Certificate Import Wizard starts, click Next.

4. On the File to Import page, type **c:\cert.bak.pfx**, and then click Next.

5. If it asks for a password, type **Pa$$w0rd** in the Password text box and click Next.

6. On the Certificate Store page, click Next.

7. On the Completing the Certificate Import Wizard page, click Finish.

8. When the import is successful, click OK.

9. Take a screen shot of the Certificates console by pressing Alt+Prt Scr and then paste it into your Lab06_worksheet file in the page provided by pressing Ctrl+V.

10. Close Certificate Manager and close the Command Prompt.

End of exercise. You can leave the windows open for the next exercise.

Exercise 6.4	Encrypting a Volume with BitLocker
Overview	In this exercise, you create a new volume and then use BitLocker to encrypt the entire volume.
Mindset	EFS will encrypt only individual files; BitLocker can encrypt an entire volume. Therefore, if you want to encrypt an entire drive on a laptop, you can use BitLocker.
Completion time	10 minutes

1. Log in to Server02 as the Contoso\Administrator user account. The Server Manager console opens.

2. On Server02, on Server Manager, click Manage and click Add Roles and Features. The Add Roles and Feature Wizard opens.

3. On the Before you begin page, click Next.

4. Select Role-based or feature-based installation and then click Next.

5. On the Select destination server page, click Next.

6. On the Select server roles page, click Next.

7. On the Select features page, select BitLocker Drive Encryption.

8. When the Add Roles and Features Wizard dialog box displays, click Add Features.

9. On the Select Features page, click Next.

10. On the Confirm installation selections page, click Install.

11. When BitLocker is installed, click Close.

12. Reboot the Server02.

13. Log in to Server02 as the Contoso\Administrator. The Server Manager console opens.

14. Using Server Manager, click Tools > Computer Management. The Computer Management console opens.

15. Expand the Storage node and click Disk Management.

16. Right-click the C drive and choose Shrink Volume.

17. In the Enter the amount of space to shrink in MB text box, type **3000** and then click Shrink.

18. Under Disk 0, right-click the unused space and click New Simple Volume.

19. When the Welcome to the New Simple Volume Wizard starts, click Next.

20. On the Specify Volume Size page, click Next.

21. On the Assign Drive Letter or Path page, click Next.

22. On the Format Partition page, click Next.

23. When the wizard is complete, click Finish.

24. Close Computer Management. If you're prompted to Format the disk, click Cancel.

25. Click the Start button and then click the Control Panel tile.

26. Click System and Security > BitLocker Drive Encryption. The BitLocker Drive Encryption window opens as shown in Figure 6-4.

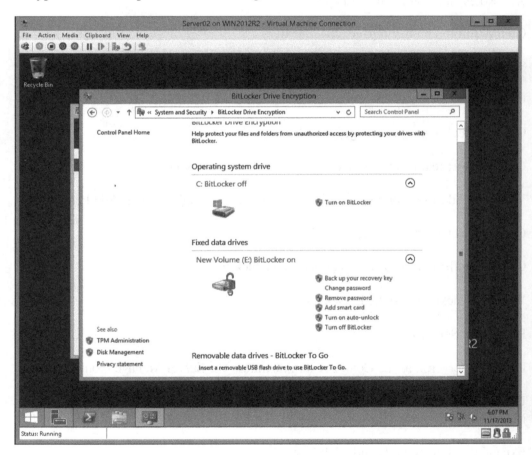

Figure 6-4
Opening the BitLocker settings

27. Click the down arrow next to the E drive. Then click Turn on BitLocker. A BitLocker Drive Encryption (E:) window opens.

28. On the Choose how you want to unlock this drive page, click to select the Use a password to unlock the drive. Type a password of **Pa$$w0rd** in the Enter your password and Reenter your password text boxes, and then click Next.

Question 12	*If you had a laptop, what chip would be used tocerate cryptographic keys and encrypted so that they can only be decrypted by the chip?*

29. On the How do you want to back up your recovery key? page, click Save to a file option.

30. When the Save BitLocker recovery key as dialog box opens, type **\\rwdc01\Software** before BitLocker Recovery Key <GUID>.txt and then click Save. Click Next.

31. On the BitLocker Drive Encryption (E:) page, select Encrypt entire drive radio button, and click Next.

32. On the Are you ready to encrypt this drive? page, click Start encrypting.

33. When the drive is encrypted, take a screen shot of the BitLocker window by pressing Alt+Prt Scr and then paste it into your Lab06_worksheet file in the page provided by pressing Ctrl+V.

34. Close the BitLocker Drive Encryption window. If you're prompted to format the disk, click Cancel.

End of exercise.

LAB REVIEW QUESTIONS

Completion time	10 minutes

1. In Exercise 6.1, how do you enable EFS?

2. In Exercise 6.1, how do you allow other users to view an EFS file that you encrypted?

3. In Exercise 6.2, how does a user get to be an EFS Recovery Agent?

4. In Exercise 6.3, what format did you use when backing up the certificates, so that it can also store the private and public keys?

5. In Exercise 6.4, what did you use to encrypt an entire volume?

6. In Exercise 6.4, from where do you control BitLocker?

Lab Challenge	Deploying Network Unlock
Overview	To complete this challenge, you will list the software components needed to implement Network Unlock and specify the server to which you would install the software component.
Mindset	You are an administrator for Contoso.com and you need to deploy Network Unlock on the Contoso network.
Completion time	10 minutes

The Contoso network included the following servers:

- RWDC01: Domain Controller and DNS Server

- Server01: DHCP Server

- Server02: Certificate Authority – Enterprise

List any other servers that you will need, list all software components that you will need to install or configure, and list where the software component will be created or installed.

End of lab.

LAB 7
CONFIGURING ADVANCED AUDIT POLICIES

THIS LAB CONTAINS THE FOLLOWING EXERCISES AND ACTIVITIES:

Exercise 7.1   Implementing Auditing

Exercise 7.2   Implementing Advanced Auditing

Exercise 7.3   Using AuditPol.exe

Lab Challenge   Auditing Removable Devices

BEFORE YOU BEGIN

The lab environment consists of student workstations connected to a local area network, along with a server that functions as the domain controller for a domain called *contoso.com*. The computers required for this lab are listed in Table 7-1.

Table 7-1
Computers Required for Lab 7

Computer	Operating System	Computer Name
Server (VM 1)	Windows Server 2012 R2	RWDC01
Server (VM 2)	Windows Server 2012 R2	Server01

In addition to the computers, you also require the software listed in Table 7-2 to complete Lab 7.

Table 7-2
Software Required for Lab 7

Software	Location
Lab 7 student worksheet	Lab07_worksheet.docx (provided by instructor)

Working with Lab Worksheets

Each lab in this manual requires that you answer questions, take screen shots, and perform other activities that you will document in a worksheet named for the lab, such as Lab07_worksheet.docx. You will find these worksheets on the book companion site. It is recommended that you use a USB flash drive to store your worksheets, so you can submit them to your instructor for review. As you perform the exercises in each lab, open the appropriate worksheet file using Word, fill in the required information, and save the file to your flash drive.

After completing this lab, you will be able to:

- Configure standard audit policies

- Configure advanced audit policies

- Using AuditPol.exe to manage audit policies

- Audit removable devices

Estimated lab time: 60 minutes

Exercise 7.1	Implementing Auditing
Overview	In this exercise, you will use standard Advanced Audit Policies to help keep track of who uses and attempts to use your network resources.
Mindset	Auditing is one of the main components of security (part of the authentication, authorization, and auditing functions). Although authentication and authorization are used to give access to resources, auditing is used to show who did what by creating records of such access.
Completion time	15 minutes

1. Log in to Server01 as Contoso\Administrator with the password of Pa$$w0rd.

2. On Server01, when the Server Manager opens, click Tools > Event Viewer. The Event Viewer console opens.

3. Expand Windows Logs and then click Security.

Question 1	*By looking at the current logs, what security events are being captured?*

4. Log in to RWDC01 as Contoso\Administrator with the password of Pa$$w0rd.

5. When Server Manger opens, click Local Server.

6. In the Properties pane, if IE Enhanced Experience Improvement Program is set to On, click On. If IE Enhanced Experience Improvement is Off, skip to Step 9.

7. When the Internet Explorer Enhanced Security Configuration dialog box opens, ensure the setting is clicked Off for the Administrators group.

8. Click OK to close the Enhanced Security Configuration dialog box.

9. Using Server Manager, click Tools > Group Policy Management. The Group Policy Management console opens.

10. Expand Forest:contoso.com\Domains\contoso.com and click Default Domain Policy. If a Group Policy Management Console dialog box opens, read the message and then click to select Do not show this message again. Click OK.

11. In the right-pane, click the Settings tab.

Question 2	*Are there any audit policy settings configured for the Default Domain Policy?*

12. Expand the Domain Controllers node and click Default Domain Controllers Policy.

13. In the right-pane, click the Settings tab.

Question 3	*Are there any audit policy settings configured for the Default Domain Controllers Policy?*

14. Right-click the contoso.com node and choose Create a GPO in this domain, and Link it here. The New GPO dialog box opens.

15. For the name, type Audit Policy and then click OK to close the New GPO dialog box.

16. Right-click the Audit Policy and choose Edit. The Group Policy Management Editor opens.

17. Expand Computer Configuration\Policies\Windows Settings\Security Settings\Local Policies and then click Audit Policy. The Policy settings display as shown in Figure 7-1.

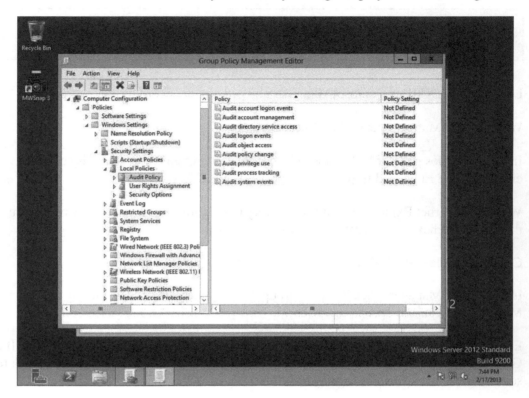

Figure 7-1
Configuring basic audit policies

18. Double-click Audit account logon events. The Audit account logon events Properties dialog box opens.

19. Click to select Define these policy settings and click to select both Success and Failure. Click OK to close the Audit account logon events Properties dialog box.

20. Double-click Audit Object access. The Audit object access Properties dialog box opens.

21. Click to select Define these policy settings and click to select both Success and Failure. Click OK to close the Audit object access Properties dialog box.

22. Take a screen shot of the Group Policy Management Editor by pressing Alt+Prt Scr and then paste it into your Lab07_worksheet file in the page provided by pressing Ctrl+V.

23. Go to Server01. Log on to unlock the screen, if needed. With the Event Viewer open and Security highlighted, press F5 to refresh the Security logs.

24. Right-click the Start button and choose Command Prompt (Admin). The Command Prompt opens.

25. Execute the following command:

```
gpupdate /force
```

26. Go back to the Event Viewer and refresh the Security logs again.

27. Take a screen shot of the Event Viewer window by pressing Alt+Prt Scr and then paste it into your Lab07_worksheet file in the page provided by pressing Ctrl+V.

Question 4	What kind of events appears now?

28. Go back to RWDC01 and log in to unlock the screen, if needed. Open both Audit object access and Audit account logon events and uncheck the Define these policy settings check boxes.

End of exercise. Leave Group Policy Management and Group Policy Management Editor open for the next exercise.

Exercise 7.2	Implementing Advanced Auditing
Overview	In this exercise, you will use Advanced Audit Policies to help keep track of who uses and attempts to use your network resources.
Mindset	Advanced auditing gives you more control over what events get recorded by using multiple subsettings instead of the traditional nine basic audit settings.
Completion time	20 minutes

1. On the RWDC01 server, ensure the Group Policy Management Editor is open.

2. In the Group Policy Management Editor on RWDC01, navigate to Computer Configuration\Policies\Windows Settings\Security Settings\Advanced Audit Policy Configuration and click Audit Policies, as shown in Figure 7-2.

Figure 7-2
Configuring Advanced Audit Policy configuration settings

3. Under Audit Policies, double-click Logon/Logoff.

4. Double-click Audit Account Lockout. When the Audit Account Lockout Properties dialog box opens, click to select Configure the following audit events, and then select Success. Click OK to close Audit Lockout Properties.

5. Configure the following settings and then click OK for each:

   Audit Logoff   Success

   Audit Logon   Success and Failure

6. Take a screen shot of the Group Policy Management Editor window by pressing Alt+Prt Scr and then paste it into your Lab07_worksheet file in the page provided by pressing Ctrl+V.

7. Under Account Policies, click Account Management and then configure the following settings:

   Audit Computer Account Management   Success and Failure

   Audit Security Group Management   Success and Failure

   Audit User Account Management   Success and Failure

8. Under Audit Policies, click Object Access and then configure the following settings:

   Audit File Share   Success and Failure

   Audit File System   Success and Failure

   Audit Registry   Success and Failure

   Audit SAM   Success and Failure

9. Click Privilege Use and then configure the following settings:

   Audit Sensitive Privilege Use   Success and Failure

10. Click System and then configure the following settings:

    Audit Security State Change   Success and Failure

11. Close the Group Policy Management Editor.

12. Go to Server01, open a Command prompt window, and then execute the **gpupdate /force** command.

End of exercise. You can leave the windows open for the next exercise.

Exercise 7.3	Using AuditPol.exe
Overview	In this exercise, you will use AuditPol.exe to manage auditing.
Mindset	You can use auditpol.exe within scripts and you can configure per-user audit policies.
Completion time	10 minutes

1. Log in to RWDC01 as contoso\administrator with the password of Pa$$w0rd. Server Manager starts.

2. Click Tools > Active Directory Users and Computers. The Active Directory Users and Computers console opens.

3. Right-click the Users node and choose New > User.

4. Create a new user with the following parameters:

   First Name: **User2**
   User logon name: **User2**
   Click Next.

5. For the Password and Confirm password text boxes, type **Pa$$w0rd**. Click to select Password never expires. When an Active Directory Domain Services dialog box appears, click OK. Click Next.

6. When the user is ready to be created, click Finish.

7. Close Active Directory Users and Computers.

8. On the RWDC01 server, open a Command Prompt and then execute the following command to get a list of all Audit settings:

```
auditpol /get /category:*
```

9. To see the audit policy set for Contoso\User2, execute the following command:

```
auditpol.exe /get /user:contoso\user2 /category:*
```

10. Observe that there is no audit policy defined for Contoso\User2. To set the audit policy for User2 so that account management is audited for User2, execute the following command:

```
auditpol.exe /set /user:contoso\user2 /subcategory:"user account
management" /success:enable /failure:enable
```

11. To display the settings for everyone again, execute the following command:

```
auditpol /get /category:*
```

12. To get the settings for user1, execute the following settings:

```
auditpol.exe /get /category:* /user:user2
```

Question 5	Are the audit policies configured with Group Policies displayed when you specified a single user?

13. Take a screen shot of the Command Prompt window by pressing Alt+Prt Scr and then paste it into your Lab07_worksheet file in the page provided by pressing Ctrl+V.

14. To reset the settings for user1, execute the following settings:

```
auditpol /remove /user:contoso\user2
```

15. Verify that the per-user setting was removed by running the following command:

```
auditpol.exe /get /user:contoso\user2 /category:*
```

End of exercise.

LAB REVIEW QUESTIONS

Completion time	10 minutes

1. In Exercise 7.1, what is the location where you would find the standard auditing settings?

2. In Exercise 7.2, what is the location where you would find the advanced auditing settings?

3. In Exercise 7.2, which category would you use to enable auditing of the Registry?

4. In Exercise 7.3, what command did you use to configure a user-based audit policy?

Lab Challenge	Auditing Removable Devices
Overview	To complete this challenge, you must demonstrate how to add audit removable devices by writing the steps to complete the tasks described in the scenario.
Mindset	When a user inserts a USB flash drive into a system, you must determine whether sensitive material is being copied onto the flash drive. What can you do?
Completion time	5 minutes

Write out the steps you performed to complete the challenge.

End of lab.

LAB 8
CONFIGURING DNS ZONES

THIS LAB CONTAINS THE FOLLOWING EXERCISES AND ACTIVITIES:

Exercise 8.1   Installing DNS

Exercise 8.2   Creating Primary and Secondary Zones

Exercise 8.3   Creating an Active Directory Integrated Zone

Exercise 8.4   Configuring Zone Delegation

Exercise 8.5   Configuring a Stub Zone

Exercise 8.6   Configuring Forwarding and Conditional Forwarding Zones

Exercise 8.7   Configuring Zone Transfers

Lab Challenge   Using the DNSCMD Command To Manage Zones

BEFORE YOU BEGIN

The lab environment consists of student workstations connected to a local area network, along with a server that functions as the domain controller for a domain called *contoso.com*. The computers required for this lab are listed in Table 8-1.

Table 8-1
Computers Required for Lab 8

Computer	Operating System	Computer Name
Server (VM 1)	Windows Server 2012 R2	RWDC01
Server (VM 2)	Windows Server 2012 R2	Server01

In addition to the computers, you also require the software listed in Table 8-2 to complete Lab 8.

Table 8-2
Software Required for Lab 8

Software	Location
Lab 8 student worksheet	Lab08_worksheet.docx (provided by instructor)

Working with Lab Worksheets

Each lab in this manual requires that you answer questions, take screen shots, and perform other activities that you will document in a worksheet named for the lab, such as Lab08_worksheet.docx. You will find these worksheets on the book companion site. It is recommended that you use a USB flash drive to store your worksheets, so you can submit them to your instructor for review. As you perform the exercises in each lab, open the appropriate worksheet file using Word, fill in the required information, and save the file to your flash drive.

After completing this lab, you will be able to:

- Configure DNS zones including primary zones, secondary zones, and Active Directory Integrated zones.

- Configure Zone delegation

- Configure a Stub Zone

- Configure Forwarding and Conditional Forwarding zones

- Configure Zone Transfers

- Use DNSCMD command to manage zones

Estimated lab time: 80 minutes

Exercise 8.1	Installing DNS
Overview	Domain Name System (DNS) is already installed on RWDC01. However, we need a second DNS server for future exercises. Therefore, during this exercise, you install a second DNS server on Server01.
Mindset	DNS is a naming service that is used by TCP/IP network and is an essential service used by the Internet. For years, Windows servers have included the DNS role.
Completion time	10 minutes

1. Log in to Server01 as the Contoso\administrator user account with the Pa$$w0rd password. The Server Manager console opens.0

2. When Server Manager opens, click Manage > Add Roles and Features.

3. On the Before you begin page, click Next.

4. Select Role-based or feature-based installation, and then click Next.

5. Click Select a server from the server pool, click Server01.contoso.com and then click Next.

6. On the Select server roles page, click DNS Server.

7. When the Add Roles and Features Wizard dialog box appears, select Add Features, and then click Next.

8. When the Select features page opens, click Next.

9. On the DNS Server page, click Next.

10. On the Confirm installation selections page, click Install.

11. When the installation is done, take a screen shot of the Add Roles and Features Wizard by pressing Alt+Prt Scr and then paste it into your Lab08_worksheet file in the page provided by pressing Ctrl+V.

12. Click **Close**.

Question 1	*For a typically large organization, how many DNS servers should you install?*

End of exercise. You can leave the windows open for the next exercise.

Exercise 8.2	Creating Primary and Secondary Zones
Overview	During this exercise, you create primary and secondary zones on RWDC01 and Server01.
Mindset	For the Contoso Corporation, you are building a new network. Therefore, you need to install DNS to support your network. You have three primary sites. When you use primary and secondary zones, you can have only one primary zone. The other sites have to be secondary zones. Therefore, you will have one primary zone and two secondary zones.
Completion time	15 minutes

Creating a Standard Forward Lookup Primary Zone

1. Log in to RWDC01 as the Contoso\administrator user account with the Pa$$word password. The Server Manager console opens.

2. On Server Manager, click Tools > DNS to open the DNS Manager console. If necessary, expand the DNS Manager console to a full-screen view.

Question 2	What is the primary tool to manage DNS in Windows?

3. Expand the server so that you can see the Forward Lookup Zones and Reverse Lookup Zones folders, if needed.

4. Click, then right-click Forward Lookup Zones and choose New Zone.

5. When the Welcome to the New Zone Wizard page opens, click Next.

6. On the Zone Type page (as shown in Figure 8-1), with the Primary zone radio button already selected, click to deselect the Store the zone in Active Directory option. Click Next.

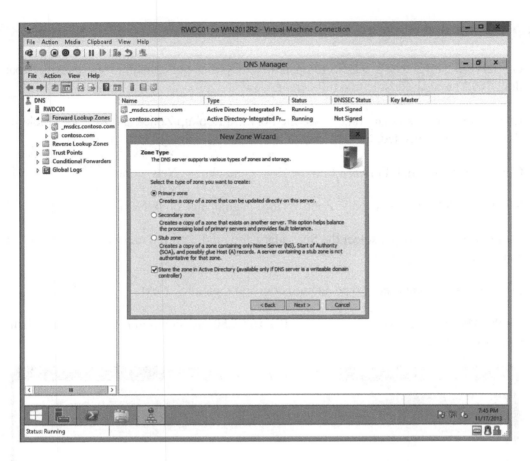

Figure 8-1
Creating a new zone

7. The Zone Name page opens. In the Zone name text box, type **adatum.com** and then click Next.

8. On the Zone File page, ensure that the Create a new file with this file name radio button is selected and then click Next.

9. On the Dynamic Update page, ensure that the Do not allow dynamic updates radio button is selected and then click Next.

10. When the Completing the New Zone Wizard page displays, take a screen shot of the New Zone wizard by pressing Alt+Prt Scr and then paste it into your Lab08_worksheet file in the page provided by pressing Ctrl+V.

11. Click Finish.

Creating a Standard Forward Lookup Secondary Zone

1. On Server01, click Tools > DNS to open the DNS Manager console. If necessary, expand the DNS Manager console to a full-screen view.

2. Expand the server so that you can see the Forward Lookup Zones and Reverse Lookup Zones folders, if needed.

3. Click, then right-click Forward Lookup Zones and choose New Zone.

4. When the Welcome to the New Zone Wizard page opens, click Next.

5. On the Zone Type page, select the Secondary zone radio button and then click Next. The Zone Name page appears.

6. In the Zone name text box, type adatum.com and then click Next.

7. On the Master DNS Servers page, type **192.168.1.50** (as shown in Figure 8-2) and then press Enter. Click Next.

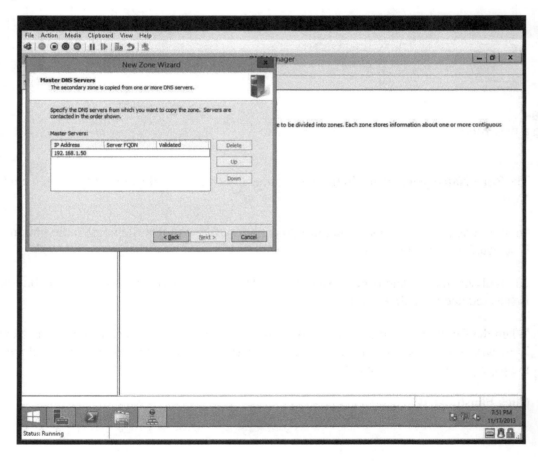

Figure 8-2
Specifying the master DNS server

8. When the Completing the New Zone Wizard page opens, click Finish.

Creating a Standard Reverse Lookup Primary Zone

1. On RWDC01, go to the DNS Manager console. Right-click Reverse Lookup Zones and choose New Zone.

2. When the Welcome to the New Zone Wizard page opens, click Next.

3. On the Zone Type page, click Next.

4. On the Active Directory Zone Replication Scope, click Next.

5. On the Reverse Lookup Zone Name page, with IPv4 Reverse Lookup Zone already selected, click Next.

6. Type the network address of **172.24.1** and then click Next.

7. On the Dynamic Update page, click Next.

8. When the Completing the New Zone Wizard page opens, take a screen shot of the New Zone Wizard by pressing Alt+Prt Scr and then paste it into your Lab08_worksheet file in the page provided by pressing Ctrl+V.

9. Click Finish.

End of exercise. You can leave the windows open for the next exercise.

Exercise 8.3	Creating an Active Directory Integrated Zone
Overview	During this exercise, you create an Active Directory Integrated zone.
Mindset	You decide that you want to improve the DNS system for your company and you are thinking of switching to Active Directory-Integrated zones. Active Directory-Integrated zones are fault tolerant, they offer better security, and they have more efficient replication. With these features, you don't have to worry about primary and secondary zones because each DNS server acts as a master.
Completion time	5 minutes

1. On RWDC01, go to the DNS Manager console.

2. Right-click the Forward Lookup Zones and choose New Zone.

3. When the Welcome to the New Zone Wizard starts, click Next.

4. With Primary zone and Store the zone in Active Directory options already selected, click Next.

5. On the Active Directory Zone Replication Scope dialog box, click Next.

6. On the Zone Name page, type **fabrikam.com** and then click Next.

7. On the Dynamic Update page, with the Allow only secure dynamic updates selected, click Next.

Question 3	*What is needed to perform secure dynamic updates?*

8. Take a screen shot of the New Zone Wizard by pressing Alt+Prt+Scr and then paste it into your Lab08_worksheet file in the page provided by pressing Ctrl+V.

9. Click Finish. The fabrikam.com domain is created.

End of exercise. You can leave the windows open for the next exercise.

Exercise 8.4	Configuring Zone Delegation
Overview	In this exercise, you delegate a subdomain called *support* under fabrikam.com on a different DNS server.
Mindset	Subdomains allow you to break up larger domains into smaller, more manageable domains. Then by using delegation, you place the subdomain on another DNS server.
Completion time	5 minutes

Question 4	*You discovered that one server is heavily utilized by many request from the support domain. What can you do to break up the workload of the server?*

1. On RWDC01, go to the DNS Manager console. Under Forward Lookup Zones, right-click Fabrikam.com and choose New Delegation.

2. When the Welcome to the New Delegation Wizard starts, click Next.

3. In the Delegated domain text box, type **support** (as shown in Figure 8-3) and then click Next.

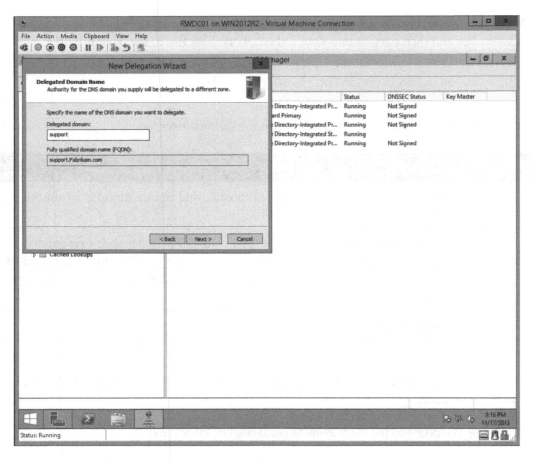

Figure 8-3
Delegating a domain

4. On the New Delegation Wizard page, click Add, type **Server01** in the Server fully qualified domain name (FQDN) text box, and then click Resolve. Ignore the red circle with the white X; the zone in Server01 still needs to be created. Click OK to close the New Name Server Record dialog box. Click Next.

5. When the wizard is complete, click Finish.

6. On Server01, go to the DNS Manager console. Right-click Forward Lookup Zones and choose New Zone.

7. When the Welcome to the New Zone Wizard starts, click Next.

8. On the Zone type, with the Primary zone already selected, click Next.

9. On the Zone Name page, type **support.fabrikam.com** in the Zone name text box and then click Next.

10. On the Zone File page, click Next.

11. On the Dynamic Update page, click Next.

12. When the wizard is complete, take a screen shot of the New Zone Wizard by pressing Alt+Prt Scr and then paste it into your Lab08_worksheet file in the page provided by pressing Ctrl+V.

13. Click Finish.

End of exercise. You can leave the windows open for the next exercise.

Exercise 8.5	Creating a Stub Zone
Overview	In this exercise, you create a stub zone that points directly to another DNS server.
Mindset	A stub zone is a copy of a zone that contains only necessary resource records—Start of Authority (SOA), Name Server (NS), and Address/Host (A) record—in the master zone and acts as a pointer to the authoritative name server.
Completion time	10 minutes

1. On RWDC01, go to the DNS Manager console. Right-click Forward Lookup Zones and choose New Zone.

2. When the Welcome to the New Zone Wizard begins, click Next.

3. When the Zone Type page opens, select the Stub zone radio button and then click Next.

Question 5	*Which feature does Stub Zones bring to DNS: better performance, redundancy, or both?*

4. On the Active Directory Zone Replication Scope page, click Next.

5. On the Zone Name page, type **litware.com** in the Zone name text box and then click Next.

6. On the Master DNS Servers page, type **192.168.1.60** and press Enter. Click Next.

7. When the Completing the New Zone Wizard displays, click Finish.

8. On Server01, go to the DNS Manager console. Right-click Forward Lookup Zones and choose New Zone.

9. When the Welcome to the New Zone Wizard begins, click Next.

10. On the Zone Type page, click Next.

11. On the Zone Name page, type **litware.com** and then click Next.

12. On the Zone File page, click Next.

13. On the Dynamic Update page, click Next.

14. When the wizard is complete, click Finish.

15. On RWDC01, click the liteware.com node and then press F5 to refresh.

16. On RWD01, take a screen shot of the DNS Manager window (with the litware.com node selected) by pressing Alt+Prt Scr and then paste it into your Lab08_worksheet file in the page provided by pressing Ctrl+V.

End of exercise. You can leave the windows open for the next exercise.

Exercise 8.6	Configuring Forwarding and Conditional Forwarding Zones
Overview	To improve performance, you can control which DNS servers requests are forwarded to when performing naming resolution by configuring forwarding and creating conditional forwarding zones. In this exercise, you configure forwarding and create a conditional forwarding zone.
Mindset	By default, when a client contacts a DNS server and the DNS server does not know the answer, it performs an iterative query to find the answer (which means it first contacts the root domain and additional DNS servers until it finds the authoritative DNS server for the zone). However, DNS servers can be configured to be forwarded to another DNS server or a conditional forwarder based on the domain name queried.
Completion time	10 minutes

Configuring Forwarders

1. On Server01, go to the DNS Manager console. Right-click Server01 and choose Properties. The Server Properties dialog box opens.

2. Select the Forwarders tab.

Question 6	*Your company uses an ISP for Internet connection. How would you relay all DNS request through the ISP DNS servers?*

3. Click Edit. The Edit Forwarders dialog box opens as shown in Figure 8-4.

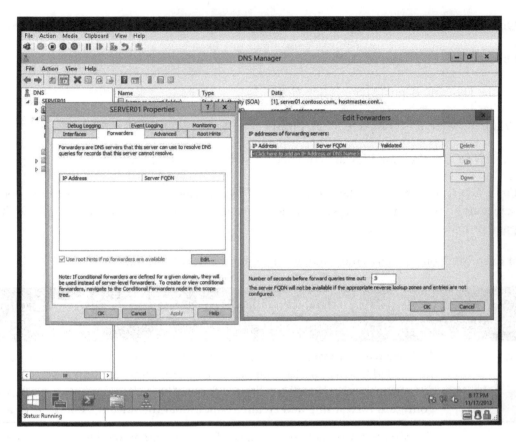

Figure 8-4
Specifying DNS servers to forward requests to

4. In the IP address column, type the **192.168.1.50** and press Enter. Click OK to close the Forwarders dialog box.

5. Click OK to close theSERVER01 Properties dialog box.

Configuring Conditional Forwarders

1. On Server01, use the DNS Manager console to create a primary lookup zone named **lucernepublishing.com**.

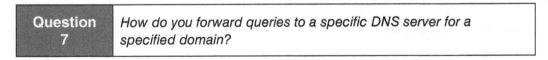

Question 7	*How do you forward queries to a specific DNS server for a specified domain?*

2. On RWDC01, go to the DNS Manager console. Click Conditional Forwarders Zones. Right-click Conditional Forwarders Zones and choose New Conditional Forwarder. The New Conditional Forwarder dialog box appears as shown in Figure 8-5.

3. Type **lucernepublishing.com** in the DNS Domain text box.

4. In the IP Address column, type **192.168.1.60** in the IP addresses column and press Enter.

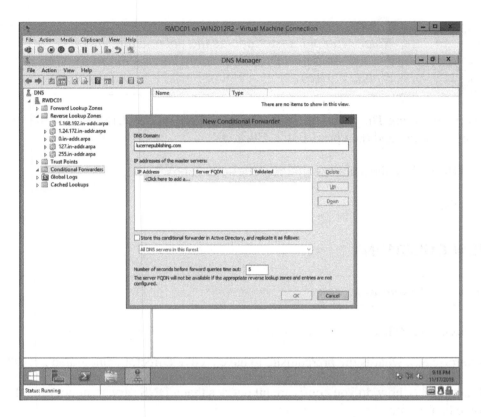

Figure 8-5
Creating a new conditional forwarder

5. Click OK to close the New Conditional Forwarder dialog box.

6. On RWDC01, with the lucernepublishing.com node selected, take a screen shot of the
    DNS Manager console by pressing Alt+Prt Scr and then paste it into your
    Lab08_worksheet file in the page provided by pressing Ctrl+V.

End of exercise. You can leave the windows open for the next exercise.

Exercise 8.7	Configuring Zone Transfers
Overview	By configuring zone transfers, you can control to which servers DNS information is copied.
Mindset	You need to configure zone transfers between multiple DNS servers. What are the three types of zone transfer available?
Completion time	10 minutes

1. On RWDC01, using the DNS Manager console, click adatum.com and then right-click
    the adatum.com zone and choose Properties. The Properties dialog box opens.

2. Click the Zone Transfers tab.

3. With the Allow zone transfers option already selected, select Only to the following
    servers radio button.

Question 8	Which type of transfer copies the entire zone, which is done when a new DNS secondary service for an existing zone is added?

4. Click Notify, click The following servers radio button, type **192.168.1.60** in the IP Address column, and then press Enter. Click OK.

5. Click OK to close the adatum.com Properties dialog box.

End of exercise.

LAB REVIEW QUESTIONS

Completion time   10 minutes

1. In Exercise 8.2, what must you create before creating the secondary zone?

2. In Exercise 8.3, what is the prerequisite to have Active Directory-Integrated zones?

3. In Exercise 8.6, how do you configure all queries that a DNS server cannot directly resolve be forwarded to your ISP's DNS server?

4. In Exercise 8.6, where did you configure forwarding?

5. In Exercise 8.7, how did you configure zone transfers?

Lab Challenge	Using the DNSCMD Command to Manage Zones
Overview	To complete this challenge, you must demonstrate how to use the DNSCMD command to manage zones.
Completion time	10 minutes

You need to configure a few scripts that will create DNS zones. Therefore, what commands would you use to perform the following on RWDC01.contoso.com:

1. Create a primary zone called fabrikam.com.

2. Create a secondary zone called contoso.com. The primary server is located at 192.168.1.60.

3. Create an Active Directory integrated zone called litware.com.

4. Delete a secondary zone called lucernpublishing.com.

5. Force a zone replication for the lucernpublishing.com zone.

End of lab.

LAB 9
CONFIGURING DNS RECORDS

THIS LAB CONTAINS THE FOLLOWING EXERCISES AND ACTIVITIES:

Exercise 9.1   Managing DNS Resource Records

Exercise 9.2   Configuring Round Robin

Exercise 9.3   Configuring Zone Scavenging

Exercise 9.4   Troubleshooting DNS

Lab Challenge   Using the DNSCMD Command to Manage Resource Records

BEFORE YOU BEGIN

The lab environment consists of student workstations connected to a local area network, along with a server that functions as the domain controller for a domain called *contoso.com*. The computers required for this lab are listed in Table 9-1.

Table 9-1
Computers Required for Lab 9

Computer	Operating System	Computer Name
Server (VM 1)	Windows Server 2012 R2	RWDC01

In addition to the computers, you also require the software listed in Table 9-2 to complete Lab 9.

Table 9-2
Software Required for Lab 9

Software	Location
Lab 9 student worksheet	Lab09_worksheet.docx (provided by instructor)

Working with Lab Worksheets

Each lab in this manual requires that you answer questions, take screen shots, and perform other activities that you will document in a worksheet named for the lab, such as Lab09_worksheet.docx. You will find these worksheets on the book companion site. It is recommended that you use a USB flash drive to store your worksheets, so you can submit them to your instructor for review. As you perform the exercises in each lab, open the appropriate worksheet file using Word, fill in the required information, and save the file to your flash drive.

After completing this lab, you will be able to:

- Manage DNS Resource Records

- Configure round robin

- Configure Zone Scavenging

- Troubleshoot DNS

- Using DNSCMD command to manage Resource Records

Estimated lab time: 60 minutes

Exercise 9.1	Managing DNS Resource Records
Overview	In the previous lab, you created several zones. With the exception of default resource records that are created when you create a zone, you need to add resource records. Therefore, during this exercise, you create resource records.
Mindset	The Host (A or AAAA) resource record is the most common resource record, which is used to resolve IP addresses from host names. However, you also need to be familiar with other common resource records (such as PTR, MX, and CNAME resource records).
Completion time	15 minutes

1. Log in to RWDC01 as the Contoso\administrator user account with the Pa$$w0rd password. The Server Manager console opens.

2. On Server Manager, click Tools > DNS to open the DNS Manager console. If necessary, expand the DNS Manager console to a full-screen view.

3. Under RWDC01, expand Forward Lookup Zones.

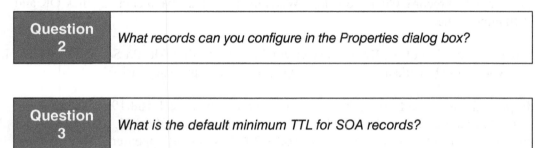

| Question 1 | What records will you find in a forward lookup zone? |

4. Right-click adatum.com and choose Properties. The Properties dialog box opens.

| Question 2 | What records can you configure in the Properties dialog box? |

| Question 3 | What is the default minimum TTL for SOA records? |

5. Click OK to close the Properties dialog box.

6. Right-click adatum.com and choose New Host (A or AAAA). The New Host dialog box opens as shown in Figure 9-1.

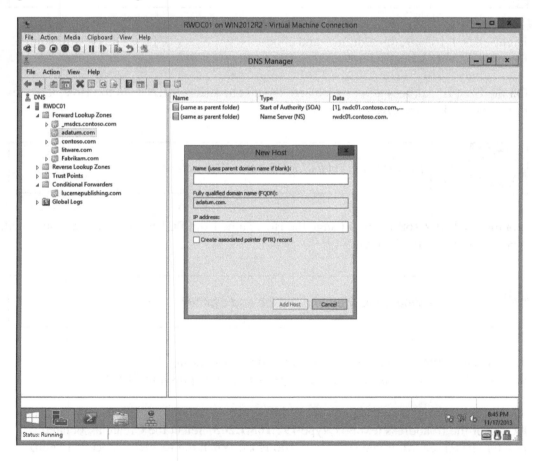

Figure 9-1
Creating a new host record

7. In the Name text box, type **PC1**. For the IP address text box, type **192.168.1.201**. Click Add Host.

8. When the record has been created, click OK and then click Done.

9. Right-click adatum.com and click New Host (A or AAAA). In the Name text box, type **PC2**. For the IP address text box, type **192.168.1.202**. Select the Create associated pointer (PTR) record. Click Add Host. When the record has been created, click OK and then click Done.

10. Take a screen shot of the DNS Manager window by pressing Alt+Prt Scr and then paste it into your Lab09_worksheet file in the page provided by pressing Ctrl+V.

11. Expand the Reverse Lookup Zones node and then click the 1.168.192.in-addr.arpa zone. Notice that the 192.168.1.202 record is there, but not the 192.168.1.201. You might need to refresh the zone if 192.168.1.202 has not yet appeared. To refresh the zone, press F5.

Question 4	What records are kept in the reverse-lookup zones?

12. Right-click 1.168.192.in-addr.arpa and choose New Pointer (PTR). The New Resource Record dialog box opens.

13. On the Host IP Address text box, change the text to **192.168.1.201**. In the Host name text box, type **PC1**. Click **OK**.

Question 5	How does the data for PC1 and PC2 differ?

14. Double-click 192.168.1.201. Change the Host name from PC1 to PC1.adatum.com. (with a period at the end). Click OK.

Question 6	What does the period at the end signify?

15. Take a screen shot of the DNS Manager window by pressing Alt+Prt Scr and then paste it into your Lab09_worksheet file in the page provided by pressing Ctrl+V.

16. Right-click adatum.com and click New Host (A or AAAA). In the Name text box, type **PC3**. For the IP address text box, type **192.168.1.203**. Select the Create associated pointer (PTR) record, if needed. Click Add Host. When the record has been created, click OK and then click Done.

17. Right-click adatum.com and choose New Alias (CNAME). In the Alias name, type **www**. In the Fully qualified domain name (FQDN) for target host text box, type **PC3.adatum.com**.

Question 7	What is the fully qualified domain name?

18. Click OK.

19. Right-click the Start button and choose Command Prompt (Admin). The Administrator: Command Prompt opens.

20. To see the name PC3 resolved to its IP address, execute the following command:

```
nslookup PC3.adatum.com
```

Question 8	What address was returned?

21. To see the IP resolution of 192.168.1.203 to its name, execute the following command:

```
nslookup 192.168.1.203
```

Question 9	What name was returned?

22. To see the resolution of the alias www.adatum.com to its name and IP address, execute the following command:

```
nslookup www.adatum.com
```

Question 10	What name and IP address was returned?

23. Right-click adatum.com and choose New Mail Exchanger (MX). In the Host or child domain text box, type **PC2**. In the Fully Qualified domain name (FQDN) of mail server, type **adatum.com**.

Question 11	What is the default Mail server priority?

24. Click OK.

25. Right-click the PC1 Host (A) record under adatum.com, and click Properties.

Question 12	What fields are displayed?

26. Click OK to close the Properties dialog box.

27. Click View > Advanced.

28. Right-click the PC1 Host (A) record and choose Properties.

Question 13	What new field is now available with the Advanced view?

29. Change the Time to live to 15 minutes.

30. Take a screen shot of the PC1 Properties dialog box by pressing Alt+Prt Scr and then paste it into your Lab09_worksheet file in the page provided by pressing Ctrl+V.

31. Click OK to close the Properties dialog box.

End of exercise. You can leave the windows open for the next exercise.

Exercise 9.2	Configuring Round Robin
Overview	By default, DNS Round Robin is enabled. Round robin operates by providing one DNS server IP address to a given query, then provides a different IP address for the next query, and so on, until a configured list of DNS server IP addresses runs out. The last query causes a loop-around to the first IP address and begins the sequence over again. In this exercise, you create two resource records to demonstate round robin switching between two separate DNS IP addresses.
Mindset	Round robin is a DNS balancing mechanism that distributes network load among multiple servers by rotating resource records retrieved from a DNS server.
Completion time	10 minutes

1. On RWDC01, with DNS Manager console, create a host record for web.adatum.com that points to 192.168.1.205.

2. Create a second host record for web.adatum.com that points to 192.168.1.206.

3. At the command prompt, execute the following command:

`nslookup web.adatum.com`

Question 14	*What addresses were returned?*

4. Re-execute the `nslookup web.adatum.com` command.

Question 15	*What addresses were returned?*

5. Execute the following command:

`ping web.adatum.com`

Don't worry that the ping fails; focus on the address that is returned.

6. Execute the `ping web.adatum.com` command again, and then execute the command a couple more times. Observe that the return address toggles back and forth between 192.168.1.205 and 192.168.1.206, in effect, balancing the query load between two IP addresses.

End of exercise. You can leave the windows open for the next exercise.

Exercise 9.3	Configuring Zone Scavenging
Overview	With dynamic addresses, often resource records will be added to a DNS zone, and will remain there unless they are manually deleted or scavanged. During this exercise, you configure zone scavenging.
Mindset	When you want DNS zone scavenging, you must enable scavenging at the server and at the zone.
Completion time	10 minutes

1. On RWDC01, with DNS Manager console, right-click **RWDC01** and choose Set Aging/Scavenging for all Zones. The Server Aging/Scavenging Properties dialog box opens as shown in Figure 9-2.

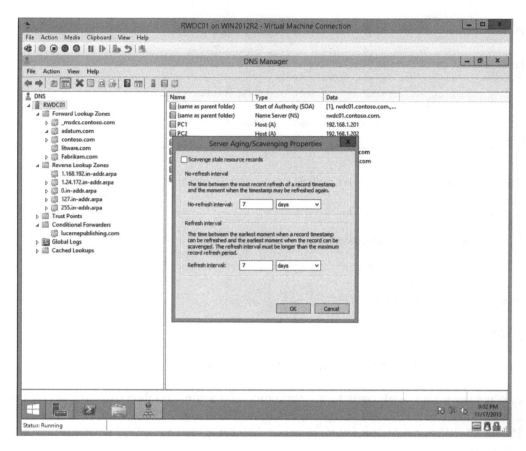

Figure 9-2
Configuring aging and scavenging settings

Question 16	*When you enable DNS scavenging, what is the default number of days before a record is scavenged?*

2. Click the Scavenge stale resource records option.

3. Click **OK** to close the Server Aging/Scavenging Properties dialog box.

4. Click to enable the Apply these settings to the existing Active Directory-integrated zones option. Click OK to close the Server Aging/Scavenging Confirmation dialog box.

5. Right-click the adatum.com zone and choose Properties.

6. On the General tab, click the Aging button. The Zone Aging/Scavenging Properties dialog box opens.

7. Click to enable the Scavenge stale resource records option.

8. Take a screen shot of the DNS Manager window by pressing Alt+Prt Scr and then paste it into your Lab09_worksheet file in the page provided by pressing Ctrl+V.

9. Click OK to close the Server Aging/Scavenging Properties dialog box.

10. When you are prompted to apply aging/scavenging settings to the Standard Primary zone, click Yes.

11. Click **OK** to close the adatum.com Properties dialog box.

End of exercise. You can leave the windows open for the next exercise.

Exercise 9.4	Troubleshooting DNS
Overview	In Exercise 9.2, you used nslookup to show name/IP resolution. However, during this exercise, you use nslookup in other ways to test DNS. You also use the DNS built-in tools to test DNS.
Mindset	Because DNS is an essential service that can bring any network down when it is not available, you need to know how to troubleshoot it. Microsoft provides several tools to help you troubleshoot DNS problems, including the IPConfig command, the NSLookup command, and the DNS console.
Completion time	10 minutes

Question 17	*What command would you use to show which DNS server a client is using?*

1. On RWDC01, at the command prompt, execute the following command:

   nslookup PC1.adatum.com

2. To start nslookup in interactive mode, execute the following command:

   nslookup

3. To display the SOA record for adatum.com domain, execute the following commands:

   set type=soa

   adatum.com

4. To display the MX record for the adatum.com domain, execute the following commands:

   set type=mx

   adatum.com

5. Take a screen shot of the Command Prompt window by pressing Alt+Prt Scr and then paste it into your Lab09_worksheet file in the page provided by pressing Ctrl+V.

6. Close the Command Prompt.

7. On RWDC01, with DNS Manager console, right-click RWDC01 and choose Properties. The properties dialog box opens.

8. Click the Monitoring tab (see Figure 9-3).

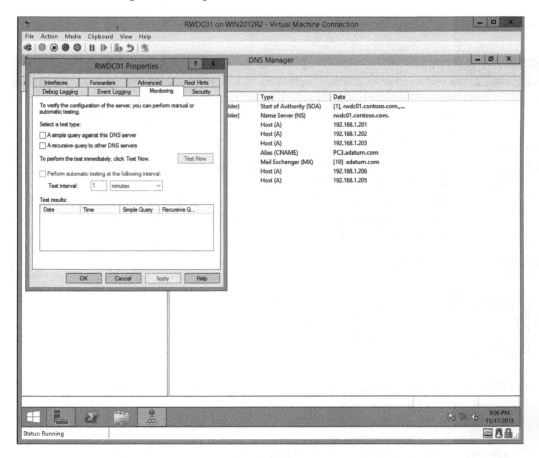

Figure 9-3
Monitoring the DNS server

9. Select to enable the following settings:

   A simple query against this DNS server

   A recursive query to other DNS servers

10. Click Test Now.

11. Take a screen shot of the RWDC01 Properties dialog box by pressing Alt+Prt Scr and then paste it into your Lab09_worksheet file in the page provided by pressing Ctrl+V.

Question 18	Did either simple query or recursive query fail? If a failure did occur, why did it fail?

12. Close DNS Manager.

LAB REVIEW QUESTIONS

Completion time	10 minutes

1. In Exercise 9.1, what is the most commonly used DNS resource record?

2. In Exercise 9.1, where is the default TTL stored?

3. In Exercise 9.1, where are PTR records stored?

4. In Exercise 9.1, what view do you need to be in to modify the TTL for an individual record?

5. In Exercise 9.2, how did you enable round robin?

6. In Exercise 9.3, to enable zone scavenging, what two places did you have to configure?

7. In Exercise 9.4, what tool is used to test DNS queries?

Lab Challenge	Using the DNSCMD Command to Manage Resource Records
Overview	To complete this challenge, you must demonstrate how to use the DNSCMD command.
Mindset	In the last lab, you were introduced to the dnscmd command to create zones. In this lesson, you can also use the dnscmd command to manage resource records.
Completion time	5 minutes

You need to configure a few scripts that will create DNS zones. What commands would you use to perform the following on RWDC01.contoso.com for the contoso.com domain:

Add a host record for Test01 with an IPv4 address of 192.168.1.221 on the RWDC01 server.

Delete the Test01 record that you just created in the previous step.

End of lab.

LAB 10
CONFIGURING VPN AND ROUTING

THIS LAB CONTAINS THE FOLLOWING EXERCISES AND ACTIVITIES:

Exercise 10.1   Installing and Configuring RRAS

Exercise 10.2   Configuring a VPN Server

Exercise 10.3   Configuring a VPN Client

Exercise 10.4   Configuring Split Tunneling

Exercise 10.5   Configuring Routing

Exercise 10.6   Resetting Servers

Lab Challenge   Using the Route Command

BEFORE YOU BEGIN

The lab environment consists of student workstations connected to a local area network, along with a server that functions as the domain controller for a domain called *contoso.com*. The computers required for this lab are listed in Table 10-1.

Table 10-1
Computers Required for Lab 10

Computer	Operating System	Computer Name
Server (VM 1)	Windows Server 2012 R2	RWDC01
Server (VM 2)	Windows Server 2012 R2	Server01
Server (VM 3)	Windows Server 2012 R2	Server02

In addition to the computers, you also require the software listed in Table 10-2 to complete Lab 10.

Table 10-2
Software Required for Lab 10

Software	Location
Lab 10 student worksheet	Lab10_worksheet.docx (provided by instructor)

Working with Lab Worksheets

Each lab in this manual requires that you answer questions, take screen shots, and perform other activities that you will document in a worksheet named for the lab, such as Lab10_worksheet.docx. You will find these worksheets on the book companion site. It is recommended that you use a USB flash drive to store your worksheets, so you can submit them to your instructor for review. As you perform the exercises in each lab, open the appropriate worksheet file using Word, fill in the required information, and save the file to your flash drive.

After completing this lab, you will be able to:

■ Install and configure Remote Access Role

■ Configure VPN settings

■ Configure routing

Estimated lab time: 125 minutes

Exercise 10.1	Installing and Configuring RRAS
Overview	To configure standard VPN connections, you use Routing and Remote Access Server. You install Routing and Remote Access Server on Server01.
Mindset	The Routing and Remote Access Server can perform Remote Access (dialup and VPN), NAT, and Routing.
Completion time	15 minutes

1. Log in to Server01 as the Contoso\administrator user account and the Pa$$w0rd password. The Server Manager console opens.

2. On Server Manager, click Manage > Add Roles and Features. The Add Roles and Feature Wizard opens.

3. On the Before you begin page, click Next.

4. Select Role-based or feature-based installation and then click Next.

5. On the Select destination server page, click Next.

6. Scroll down and select Remote Access and then click Next.

7. On the Select features page, click Next.

8. On the Remote Access page, click Next. On the Select role services page, select DirectAccess and VPN (RAS).

9. When the Add Roles and Features Wizard dialog box opens, click Add Features.

10. On the Select role services page, select Routing and then click Next.

11. If the Web Server Role (IIS) page appears, click Next twice.

12. On the Confirm installation selections page, click Install.

13. Take a screen shot of the Remote Access Installation progress page by pressing Alt+Prt Scr and then paste it into your Lab10_worksheet file in the page provided by pressing Ctrl+V.

Question 1	*You have a user who will be giving demonstrations of your company products while traveling to the customer sites. For the demonstrations to work, the user will need to access the corporate servers and files. What should you install and configure?*

14. When the installation is complete, click Close.

End of exercise. You can leave the windows open for the next exercise.

Exercise 10.2	Configuring a VPN Server
Overview	Server01 will be the primary application server, which will be used for most applications.
Mindset	The types of VPN connections that are supported by Routing and Remote Access Server include PPTP, L2TP, IKEv2, and SSTP
Completion time	30 minutes

1. On Server01, on the Task bar, right-click the Network and Sharing Center icon and choose Open Network and Sharing Center.

2. Click Change adapter settings.

3. Right-click the first Ethernet connection3 and choose Rename. Change the name to **Internal** and then press Enter.

4. Right-click second Ethernet conneciton and choose Rename. Change the name to **External** and then press Enter.

5. Right-click External and choose Properties.

6. When the External Properties dialog box opens, double-click Internet Protocol Version 4 (TCP/IPv4).

7. Click Use the following IP address and specify the following:

   IP address: **192.168.2.1**

   Subnet mask: **255.255.255.0**

   Click OK. If a message indicates the DNS server list is empty, click OK.

8. Click OK to close the External Properties dialog box.

9. Close Network Connections.

10. On Server01, Server Manager, click Tools > Routing and Remote Access. The Routing and Remote Access console opens as shown in Figure 10-1.

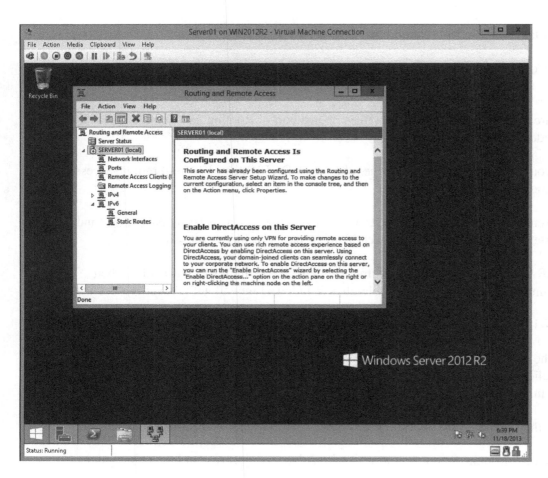

Figure 10-1
Opening the Routing and Remote Access console

11. Right-click Server01 and choose Configure and Enable Routing and Remote Access. The Routing and Remote Access Server Setup Wizard opens.

12. On the Welcome page, click Next.

13. On the Configuration page, select Virtual private network (VPN) access and NAT and then click Next.

14. On the VPN Connection page, select External and then click Next.

15. On the IP Address Assignment page, click From a specified range of addresses and then click Next.

16. On the Address Range Assignment page, click New.

17. When the New IPv4 Address Range dialog box opens, specify the Start IP address as **192.168.1.40** and the End IP address as **192.168.1.45**. Click OK.

18. Back on the Address Range Assignment page, click Next.

19. On the Managing Multiple Remote Access Servers page, click Next.

20. On the Completing the Routing and Remote Access Server Setup Wizard page, click Finish.

21. If you are alerted to the fact that you must open a port of Routing and Remote access in the Windows Firewall, click OK.

22. When you are prompted to support the relaying of DHCP messages from remote access clients message, click OK.

23. Take a screen shot of the Routing and Remote Access window by pressing Alt+Prt Scr and then paste it into your Lab10_worksheet file in the page provided by pressing Ctrl+V.

24. After RRAS starts, click the Start button and then click Administrative Tools. When theAdministrative Tools opens, double-click Windows Firewall with Advanced Security.

25. When Windows Firewall with Advanced Security opens, under Actions, click Properties.

26. When the Windows Firewall with Advanced Security on Local Computer dialog box opens, click the Windows Firewall Properties link at the bottom of the Overview pane, then change the Domain Profile Firewall state to Off.

27. Change the Firewall state to Off in the Private profile and Public Profile tabs.

28. Click OK to close the Windows Firewall with Advanced Security on Local Computer dialog box.

29. Close Windows Firewall with Advanced Security and close the Administrative Tools.

30. In Routing and Remote Access, right-click Server01 and choose Properties.

Question 2	Which tab would you use to specify a preshared key for RRAS?

Question 3	Which VPN method requires a digital ceritificate to provide a SSL connection?

31. Click OK to close the SERVER01 (local) Properties dialog box.

32. Right-click Ports and choose Properties. The Ports Properties dialog box opens.

Question 4	By default, how many IKEv2 connections are available?

33. Click OK to close the Ports Properties dialog box.

34. Log on to RWDC01 as Contoso\Administrator and the Pa$$w0rd password.

35. On Server Manager, click Tools > Active Directory Users and Computers.

36. Expand contoso.com, if needed, and then click Users.

37. Double-click the Administrator account. The Administrator Properties dialog box opens.

38. Click the Dial-in tab.

Question 5	What is the default setting for Network Access Permission?

39. In the Network Access Permission section, click to select Allow access.

40. Take a screen shot of the Administrator Properties dialog box by pressing Alt+Prt Scr and then paste it into your Lab10_worksheet file in the page provided by pressing Ctrl+V.

41. Click OK to close the Administrator Properties dialog box.

42. Close Active Directory Users and Computers.

End of exercise. You can leave the windows open for the next exercise.

Exercise 10.3	Configuring a VPN Client
Overview	Now that you have configured the VPN server, you need to configure a client to connect to the VPN server. During this exercise, you use Server02 to act as a VPN client.
Mindset	To connect to a VPN connection using the built-in tools that comes with Windows 8, you have to use the Network and Sharing Center to create a new workplace connection.
Completion time	30 minutes

1. Log in to Server02 as the Contoso\Administrator user account with the Pa$$w0rd password. The Server Manager console opens.

2. On Server02, on the Taskbar, right-click Network and Sharing Center icon and choose Open Network and Sharing Center.

3. Click Change adapter settings.

4. Right-click first Ethernet connection and choose Disable.

5. Right-click the second Ethernet connection and choose Properties.

6. When the Ethernet Properties dialog box opens, double-click Internet Protocol Version 4 (TCP/IPv4).

7. Click Use the following IP address option and specify the following:

   IP address: **192.168.2.10**

   Subnet mask: **255.255.255.0**

   Click OK.

8. Click OK to close the Ethernet 4 Properties dialog box.

9. Go back to Network and Sharing Center, and choose Set up a new connection or network.

10. On the Set Up a Connection or Network page, choose Connect to a workplace and then click Next.

11. On the Connect to a Workplace page, click Use my Internet connection.

12. If you are prompted to set up Internet connection, click I'll set up an Internet connection later.

13. When you are prompted to type the Internet address to connect to, type **192.168.2.1** in the Internet address text box and then click Create.

14. When the Networks pane appears (as shown in Figure 10-2), click VPN Connection and then click Connect.

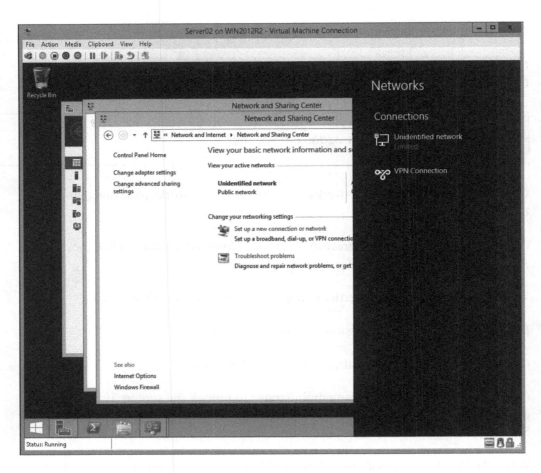

Figure 10-2
Clicking VPN Connection

15. For the user name and password, use Contoso\Administrator and Pa$$w0rd.
    Click OK.

16. Take a screen shot of the Networks pane showing a successful connection by pressing
    Alt+Prt Scr and then paste it into your Lab10_worksheet file in the page provided by
    pressing Ctrl+V.

17. Click the VPN Connection and then click Disconnect.

18. Click the Desktop.

19. On RWDC01, using Active Directory Users and Computers, double-click the
    Administrator account in the Users container.

20. When the Administrator Properties dialog box opens, click the Dial-in tab.

21. In the Network Access Permission section, click Control access through NPS
    Network Policy.

22. Click OK to close the Administrator Properties dialog box.

23. On Server02, click the Network and Sharing Center icon on the taskbar, click VPN Connection, and then click Connect.

Question 6	What error message did you get?

24. Click the left arrow next to Networks at the top of the Networks pane and then click the Desktop.

25. On RWDC01, using Active Directory Users and Computers, double-click the Administrator account.

26. When the Administrator Properties dialog box opens, click the Dial-in tab.

27. In the Network Access Permission section, click Allow access.

28. Click OK to close the Administrator Properties dialog box.

29. On Server01, log in as Contoso\administrator to unlock the screen, if needed, then open the Administrative Tools and double-click Windows Firewall with Advanced Security.

30. When the Windows Firewall with Advanced Security console opens, click Properties under Actions.

31. On the Domain Profile tab, change the Firewall state to On.

32. Using the Private Profile and Public Profile tabs, turn the Firewall state to On.

33. Click OK to close the Windows Firewall with Advanced Security on Local Computer dialog box and then close the Windows Firewall with Advanced Security window.

34. On Server02, click the Open Network and Sharing Center icon on the taskbar.

35. Click VPN Connection and then click Connect.

Question 7	What error message did you get?

36. Click the left arrow next to Networks at the top of the Networks pane and then click the Desktop.

37. On Server01, using Windows Firewall with Advanced Security, click Properties under Actions.

38. On the Domain Profile tab, change the Firewall state to Off.

39. Using the Private Profile and Public Profile tabs, turn the Firewall state to Off.

40. Click OK to close the Windows Firewall with Advanced Security on Local Computer console.

Question 8	Besides using the built-in networking tools found in Windows, what can you use to create an executable that will automatically create a VPN client to connect to a particular server or address?

End of exercise. You can leave the windows open for the next exercise.

Exercise 10.4	Configuring Split Tunneling
Overview	During this exercise, you take the current VPN connection that you created in Exercise 10.3, and enable split tunneling, so that corporate traffic will go through the Internet and Internet traffic will go out the local Internet connection.
Mindset	By using split tunneling, Internet traffic does not go through the corporate network and the corporate firewalls and proxy servers. As a result, traffic is not filtered, which might allow malware into the corporate network if the client computer is infected with the malware.
Completion time	5 minutes

1. On Server02, right-click the Network icon on the taskbar, choose Open Network and Sharing Center, and then click Change Adapter settings.

2. In the Network Connections window, right-click VPN Connection and choose Properties. The VPN Connection Properties dialog box opens.

3. Click the Networking tab.

4. Double-click the Internet Protocol Version 4 (TCP/IPv4).

5. On the Internet Protocol Version 4 (TCP/IPv4) Properties dialog box, click the Advanced button.

6. On the Advanced TCP/IP Settings dialog box, on the IP Settings tab, deselect Use default gateway on remote network.

7. Take a screen shot of the Advanced TCP/IP Settings dialog box by pressing Alt+Prt Scr and then paste it into your Lab10_worksheet file in the page provided by pressing Ctrl+V.

8. Click OK to close the Advanced TCP/IP Settings dialog box.

9. Click OK to close the Internet Protocol Version 4 (TCP/IPv4) Properties dialog box.

10. Click OK to close the VPN Connection Properties dialog box.

Question 9	*You have an executuve who needs to download video's. His home Internet connection is faster than the corporate network. Therefore, when he is at home, he would like to download the video's using this Internet connection when connected to the corporate office through a VPN connection. What can you do?*

End of exercise. You can leave the windows open for the next exercise.

Exercise 10.5	Configuring Routing
Overview	During this exercise, you configure one of the more basic routing protocols to Server01.
Mindset	The only dynamic routing protocol that is available with Windows Server 2012 is Routing Information Protocol (RIP). Although RIP requires almost no configuration after installation, it has a limit of 15 hops. Anything that is more than 15 hops is considered unreachable.
Completion time	20 minutes

1. On Server02, right-click the Network and Sharing Center icon on the taskbar and choose Open Network and Sharing Center.

2. When the Network and Sharing Center opens, click the Change adapter settings link and then double-click the second Ethernet connection.

3. When the Ethernet Status dialog box opens, click Properties.

4. When the Ethernet Properties dialog box opens, double-click Internet Protocol Version 4 (TCP/IPv4).

5. In the Internet Protocol Version 4 (TCP/IPv4) Properties dialog box, configure the Default gateway to **192.168.2.1**.

6. Click OK to close the Internet Protocol Version 4 (TCP/IPv4) Properties dialog box.

7. Click OK to close the Ethernet 4 Properties dialog box. If the Networks pane opens, prompting you to find PCs, devices, and content…, click No.

8. Click Close to close the Ethernet 4 Status dialog box.

9. Open a command prompt and try to ping 192.168.1.60.

Question 10	*Did the ping succeed?*

10. On Server01, using Routing and Remote Access, right-click Server01 (local) and choose Disable Routing and Remote Access.

11. When you are prompted to continue, click Yes. It will take a couple minutes to stop Routing and Remote Access.

12. Right-click Server01 and choose Configure and Enable Routing and Remote Access.

13. When the Routing and Remote Access Server Setup Wizard starts, click Next.

14. On the Configuration page, click Custom configuration and then click Next.

15. On the Custom Configuration page, click to select LAN routing and then click Next.

16. When the wizard is complete, click Finish.

17. When the Routing and Remote Access dialog box opens, click Start service.

18. Expand the IPv4 node. Then right-click General under IPv4 and choose New Routing Protocol.

19. When the New Routing Protocol dialog box opens (as shown in Figure 10-3), click RIP Version2 for Internet Protocol and then click OK.

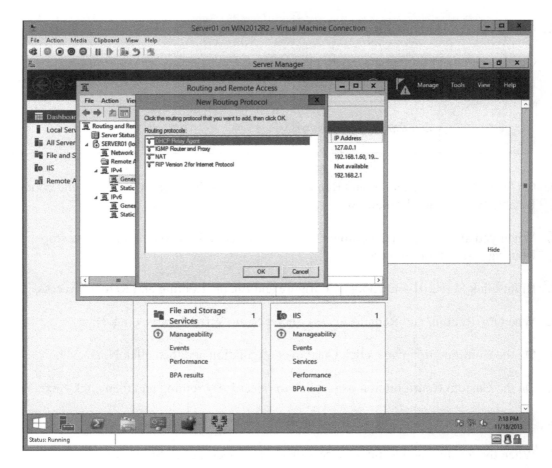

Figure 10-3
Adding a new routing protocol

20. Right-click RIP and choose New Interface.

21. Click External and then click OK.

22. When the RIP Properties – External Properties dialog box opens, click OK.

23. Right-click RIP and choose New Interface.

24. Click Internal and then click OK.

25. When the RIP Properties – Internal Properties dialog box opens, click OK.

26. On Server02, using the command prompt, execute the following command:

```
Ping 192.168.1.6
```

Question 11	Did the ping succeed?

End of exercise. You can leave the windows open for the next exercise.

Exercise 10.6	Resetting Servers
Overview	Before you can continue to the next exercise, you need to disable Routing and Remote Access.
Mindset	If you no longer need to have remote access, VPN, or NAT available on a Windows server, you can disable Routing and Remote Access.
Completion time	5 minutes

1. On Server01, with Routing and Remote Access, right-click Server01 and choose Disable Routing and Remote Access.

2. When you are prompted to continue, click Yes.

3. After RRAS stops, close Routing and Remote Access.

4. On Server02, open Network and Sharing Center, if needed.

5. Click Change adapter settings.

6. Right-click the first Ethernet connection and choose Enable.

7. Close Network Connections and Network and Sharing Center.

LAB REVIEW QUESTIONS

Completion time	10 minutes

1. In Exercise 10.2, what software included with Windows Server 2012 allows you to create a VPN server used with PPTP and L2TP?

2. In Exercise 10.2, what program did you use to allow the Administrator to connect using RRAS?

3. In Exercise 10.3, where do you define VPN connections in Windows Server 2012 when a server needs to act as a VPN client?

4. In Exercise 10.4, which option was used to enable or disable split tunneling?

5. In Exercise 10.5, what version of RIP does Windows Server 2012 support?

Lab Challenge	Using the Route Command
Overview	To complete this challenge, you will demonstrate how to use the Route command.
Mindset	By default, routes are automatically created within Windows. However, you can create static routes by using the route.exe command.
Completion time	10 minutes

Specify the commands that you would use to perform the following tasks:

1. What command would you to display the routing table in Windows?

2. What command would you to create a route to the 172.25.1.x (mask 255.255.255.0) that goes out the 192.168.1.20 router?

3. What option makes a static router permanent so that the route will remain after a computer is rebooted?

4. What command would use to delete the route defined in Question 2?

End of lab.

LAB 11
CONFIGURING
DirectAccess

THIS LAB CONTAINS THE FOLLOWING EXERCISES AND ACTIVITIES:

Exercise 11.1   Implementing Client Configuration

Exercise 11.2   Implementing DirectAccess Server

Exercise 11.3   Implementing the Infrastructure Servers

Exercise 11.4   Implementing the Application Servers

Exercise 11.5   Resetting Servers

Lab Challenge   Configuring Certificates for DirectAccess

BEFORE YOU BEGIN

The lab environment consists of student workstations connected to a local area network, along with a server that functions as the domain controller for a domain called *contoso.com*. The computers required for this lab are listed in Table 11-1.

Table 11-1
Computers Required for Lab 11

Computer	Operating System	Computer Name
Server (VM 1)	Windows Server 2012 R2	RWDC01
Server (VM 2)	Windows Server 2012 R2	Server01

In addition to the computers, you also require the software listed in Table 11-2 to complete Lab 11.

Table 11-2
Software Required for Lab 11

Software	Location
Lab 11 student worksheet	Lab11_worksheet.docx (provided by instructor)

Working with Lab Worksheets

Each lab in this manual requires that you answer questions, take screen shots, and perform other activities that you will document in a worksheet named for the lab, such as Lab11_worksheet.docx. You will find these worksheets on the book companion site. It is recommended that you use a USB flash drive to store your worksheets, so you can submit them to your instructor for review. As you perform the exercises in each lab, open the appropriate worksheet file using Word, fill in the required information, and save the file to your flash drive.

After completing this lab, you will be able to:

■ Configure DirectAccess

■ Prepare for DirectAccess Deployment

■ Configure certificates for DirectAccess

Estimated lab time: 50 minutes

Exercise 11.1	Implementing Client Configuration
Overview	To implement DirectAccess, the installation and configuration is divided into four steps. During this exercise, you perform Step 1 - Client Configuration.
Mindset	The minimum requirements for the DirectAccess serve is that the DirectAccess server must be part of the domain and be running Windows Server 2008 R2 or higher. It also must use IPv6 or some sort of IPv6 to IPv4 technology.
Completion time	10 minutes

1. Log in to Server01 as the Contoso\Administrator user account and the Pa$$w0rd password. The Server Manager console appears.

2. On Server Manager, click Tools > Remote Access Management. The Remote Access Management Console opens as shown in Figure 11-1.

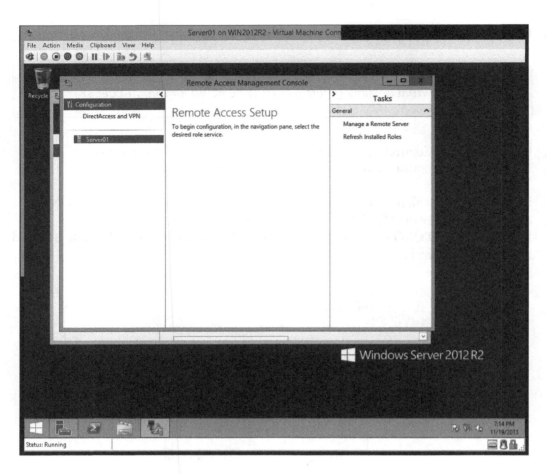

Figure 11-1
Opening the Remote Access Management Console

3. Click the DirectAccess and VPN link in the navigation pane.

4. When the Configure Remote Access wizard starts, click the Run the Getting Started Wizard link and then click the Deploy DirectAccess only option. The Remote Access Setup console opens.

5. When you are prompted to select the network topology, select Behind an edge device (with two network adapters). In the text box, type **server01.contoso.com** and then click Next.

6. On the Remote Access settings will be applied page, click Finish.

7. Take a screen shot of the Applying Getting Started Wizard Settings dialog box by pressing Alt+Prt Scr and then paste it into your Lab11_worksheet file in the page provided by pressing Ctrl+V.

8. When The configuration was applied successfully with warnings message appears, click Close.

9. Under Step 1, Remote Clients, click **Edit**. The DirectAccess Client Setup Wizard opens.

10. On the Deployment Scenario page, select Deploy full DirectAccess for client access and remote management and then click Next.

11. On the Select Groups page, answer the following question and then click Next.

Question 1	*What security group is already selected for DirectAccess?*

12. On the Network Connectivity Assistant page, click the http://directaccess-WebProbeHost.contoso.com entry and then press Delete.

13. Double-click a blank resource space. In the Configure Corporate Resources for NCA dialog box, change the HTTP to PING and, in the text box, type **RWDC01.CONTOSO.COM**. Click Add. RWDC01.CONTOSO.COM should be listed as shown in Figure 11-2.

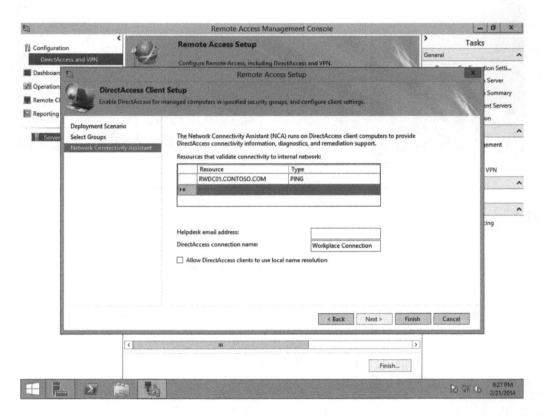

Figure 11-2
Configure the Network Connectivity Assistant

Question 2	*What tool is included with Windows 8 that will help you connect to the DirectAccess server when you have problems and can be used to perform diagnostics for client access to Direct Access?*

14. On the Network Connectivity Assistant page, click Finish.

End of exercise. Leave Remote Access Management console open for the next exercise.

Exercise 11.2	Implementing DirectAccess Server
Overview	During this exercise, you configure DirectAccess configuration Step 2 - Configuring the Remote Access Server.
Mindset	When you configure DirectAccess, you must choose the network topology and configure the network connections. In addition, you might also configure the use of smart cards.
Completion time	10 minutes

1. On Server01, using Remote Access Management console, under Step 2, Remote Access Server, click **Edit**. The Remote Access Server Setup wizard starts.

2. On the Network Topology page click Next.

3. On the Network Adapters page, select External for the Adapter connected to the external network and then select Internal for the Adapter connected to the internal network.

4. Click to select the Use a self-signed certificate created automatically by DirectAccess. Click Next.

5. On the Authentication page, with Active Directory credentials (username/password) already selected, click Finish.

Question 3	*What type of user authentication is selected by default?*

End of exercise. Leave Remote Access Management console open for the next exercise.

Exercise 11.3	Implementing the Infrastructure Servers
Overview	During this exercise, you perform Step 3, where you specify the infrastructure servers that are necessary for DirectAccess to function properly.
Mindset	In Step 3, you specify the core infrastructure services, such as Active Directory domain controllers and DNS servers. You also configure the location services. You also specify your management servers, such as Windows Update servers and anti-virus management servers.
Completion time	10 minutes

1. On Server01, continuing with the Remote Access Setup Configuration page, under Step 3, Infrastructure Servers, click Edit. The Infrastructure Server Setup Wizard starts.

2. On the Network Location Server page, click The network location server is deployed on the Remote Access server and then click to select the Use a self-signed certificate.

3. Take a screen shot of the Infrastructure Server Setup window by pressing Alt+Prt Scr and then paste it into your Lab11_worksheet file in the page provided by pressing Ctrl+V.

4. Click Next.

5. On the DNS page, click Next.

6. On the DNS Suffix Search List page, click Next.

7. On the Management page, double-click the first line of the Management Servers box to open the Add a Management Server dialog box.

Question 4	Which management servers would you include?

8. In the Computer name text box, type **rwdc01.contoso.com** and then click OK.

9. Click Finish.

End of exercise. Leave Remote Access Management console open for the next exercise.

Exercise 11.4	Implementing the Application Servers
Overview	Lastly, during Step 4, you need to configure any application servers and apply all the changes that you have configured for Steps 1 through 4.
Mindset	In Step 4, you can choose additional security features, such as extending authentication to an application server, or you can specify which individual servers require secure connections.
Completion time	5 minutes

1. On Server01, continuing with the Remote Access Setup Configuration page, under Step 4, Application Servers, click Edit. The DirectAccess Application Server Setup wizard starts.

Question 5	Which step would you use to provide secure connectin with individual severs that you want to establish esecure connnections with?

2. On the DirectAccess Application Server Setup page, click Finish, accepting the default option selected – Do not extend authentication to application servers.

3. At the bottom of the Remote Access Management console, click Finish to apply all the changes for Steps 1 through 4.

4. Take a screen shot of the Remote Access Review window by pressing Alt+Prt Scr and then paste it into your Lab11_worksheet file in the page provided by pressing Ctrl+V.

5. On the Remote Access Review window, click Apply.

6. When the settings have been applied, leave the Remote Access Management Console open for the next exercise.

End of exercise.

Exercise 11.5	Resetting Servers
Overview	Before you can continue to the next exercise, you need to disable DirectAccess.
Mindset	To stop DirectAccess, you should remove the DirectAccess configuration from the server.
Completion time	5 minutes

1. On Server01, using Remote Access Management Console, under Tasks, click Remove Configuration Settings.

2. In the Confirm Remove Configuration dialog box, click OK.

3. After the configuration removal is applied successfully, click Close.

4. Close the Remote Access Management Console.

5. Open the Network and Sharing Center and then click Change adapter settings.

6. Right-click the External adapter and choose Disable.

7. Close the Network Connections and Network and Sharing Center windows.

End of exercise.

LAB REVIEW QUESTIONS

Completion time   5 minutes

1. In Exercise 11.1, what tool is used to configure DirectAccess?

2. In Exercise 11.2, in which step did you specify the certificate authority?

3. In Exercise 11.3, what is the function of the Network Location Server?

Lab Challenge	Configuring Certificates for DirectAccess
Overview	To complete this challenge, you will demonstrate how to configure certificates for DirectAccess by writing the high-level steps to complete the tasks described in the scenerio.
Mindset	For DirectAccess to function, you must install and configure a Certificate Authority so that it can distribute digital certificates to the clients. You also need to install and configure digital certificates for the IP-HTTPS listener.
Completion time	10 minutes

Explain the general steps needed to configure the certificate requirements needed for DirectAccess.

End of lab.

LAB 12
CONFIGURING A NETWORK POLICY SERVER

THIS LAB CONTAINS THE FOLLOWING EXERCISES AND ACTIVITIES

Exercise 12.1   Installing and Configuring Network Policy Server

Exercise 12.2   Configuring NPS for RADIUS Server for VPN Connections

Exercise 12.3   Managing RADIUS Templates

Exercise 12.4   Configuring RADIUS Accounting

Lab Challenge   Add Workstation Authentication Certificates to All Workstations

BEFORE YOU BEGIN

The lab environment consists of student workstations connected to a local area network, along with a server that functions as the domain controller for a domain called *contoso.com*. The computers required for this lab are listed in Table 12-1.

Table 12-1
Computers Required for Lab 12

Computer	Operating System	Computer Name
Server (VM 1)	Windows Server 2012 R2	RWDC01
Server (VM 2)	Windows Server 2012 R2	Server01

In addition to the computers, you also require the software listed in Table 12-2 to complete Lab 12.

Table 12-2
Software Required for Lab 12

Software	Location
Lab 12 student worksheet	Lab12_worksheet.docx (provided by instructor)

Working with Lab Worksheets

Each lab in this manual requires that you answer questions, shoot screen shots, and perform other activities that you will document in a worksheet named for the lab, such as Lab12_worksheet.docx. You will find these worksheets on the book companion site. It is recommended that you use a USB flash drive to store your worksheets, so you can submit them to your instructor for review. As you perform the exercises in each lab, open the appropriate worksheet file using Word, fill in the required information, and save the file to your flash drive.

After completing this lab, you will be able to:

- Install and configure Network Policy Server

- Configure RADIUS clients

- Manage RADIUS templates

- Configure RADIUS accounting

Estimated lab time: 65 minutes

Exercise 12.1	Installing and Configuring Network Policy Server
Overview	In this exercise, you install and configure Microsoft's RADIUS server known as Network Policy Server
Mindset	The Network Policy Server is used as Microsoft's RADIUS server. It provides centralized authentication for RADIUS clients such as VPN servers and wireless access points. It also provides accounting information to log files on the local hard disk or in a Microsoft SQL Server database for those clients.
Completion time	15 minutes

Installing Network Policy and Access Services

1. Log in to RWDC01 as the Contoso\Administrator user account and the **Pa$$w0rd** password. The Server Manager console opens.

2. On Server Manager, click Manage > Add Roles and Features. The Add Roles and Features Wizard opens.

3. On the Before you begin page, click Next.

4. Select Role-based or feature-based installation and then click Next.

5. On the Select destination server page, click Next.

6. On the Select server roles page, select Network Policy and Access Services.

7. When you are prompted to add features that are required for Network Policy and Access Services, click Add Features.

8. Back on the Select server roles page, click Next.

9. On the Select features page, click Next.

10. On the Network Policy and Access Services page, click Next.

11. On the Select role services page, with the Network Policy Server selected, click Next.

12. On the Confirm installation page, click **Install**.

13. When the installation is complete, click Close.

Adding a Remote RADIUS Server Group

1. On RWDC01, with Server manager, click Tools > Network Policy Server. The Network Policy Server console opens (see Figure 12-1).

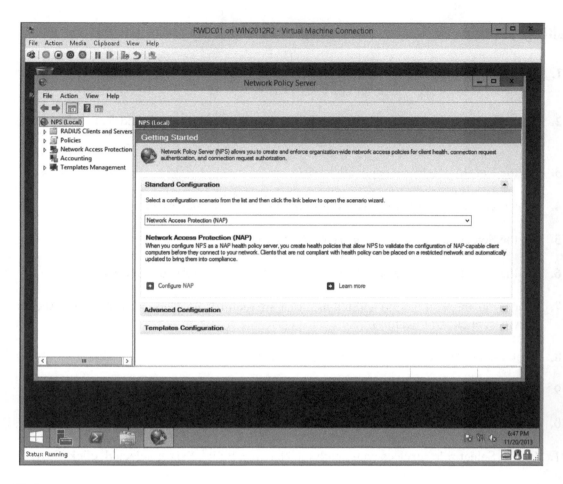

Figure 12-1
Network Policy Server console

2. Expand the Network Policy Server console to fill the entire screen.

3. In the NPS (Local) tree, double-click RADIUS Clients and Servers, then right-click Remote RADIUS Server Groups and choose New. The New Remote RADIUS Server Group dialog box opens.

4. In Group name, type **RADIUS Servers** in Group name text box and then click Add. The Add RADIUS Server dialog box opens.

5. In the Add RADIUS Server dialog box, in the Server text box, type the IP address of RWDC01, **192.168.1.50**.

6. Click the Authentication/Accounting tab.

Question 1	What is the default authentication port used with RADIUS servers?

Question 2	*What is the default accounting port used with RADIUS servers?*

7. Take a screen shot of the Add RADIUS Server dialog box by pressing Alt+Prt Scr and then paste it into your Lab12_worksheet file in the page provided by pressing Ctrl+V.

8. Click OK to close the Add RADIUS Server dialog box.

Question 3	*What is the default weight assigned to the new RADIUS server?*

9. Click OK to close the New Remote RADIUS Server group.

End of exercise. Leave the Network Policy Server console open for the next exercise.

Exercise 12.2	Configuring NPS for RADIUS Server for VPN Connections
Overview	During this exercise, you configure NPS to support VPN connections.
Mindset	RADIUS clients (also referred to as access servers) are servers (such as servers running RRAS) and devices (such as wireless access points and 802.1X switch) that forward RADIUS requests to a RADIUS server. An access client is a computer or device that contacts or connects to a RADIUS client, which requires authentication and authorization to connect.
Completion time	10 minutes

1. On RWDC01, using the Network Policy Server console, click NPS (Local).

2. Use the down arrow under Standard Configuration in the main panel, and select RADIUS server for Dial-Up or VPN Connections.

3. Click Configure VPN or Dial-Up. The Configure VPN or Dial-Up wizard opens.

4. On the Select Dial-up or Virtual Private Network Connections Type page, select Virtual Private Network (VPN) Connections and then click Next.

5. On the Specify Dial-Up or VPN Server page, click Add.

6. When the New RADIUS Client dialog box opens, type **Server01** in the Friendly name text box. In the Address (IP or DNS) text box, type **192.168.1.60**.

7. At the bottom of the dialog box, type **Pa$$w0rd** in the Shared secret and Confirm shared secret text box. Click OK to close the New RADIUS Client dialog box.

8. On the Specify Dial-Up or VPN Server page, click Next.

9. On the Configure Authentication Methods page, answer the following question.

Question 4	By default, what was the authentication method selected?

10. Take a screen shot of the Configure Authentication Methods page by pressing Alt+Prt Scr and then paste it into your Lab12_worksheet file in the page provided by pressing Ctrl+V.

11. Click Next. On the Specify User Groups page, answer the following question and click Next.

Question 5	What happens if you do not define a user group?

12. On the Specify IP Filters page, click Next.

13. On the Specify Encryption Settings page, click Next.

14. On the Specify a Realm Name page, type **contoso.com** in the Realm name field and then click Next.

15. When the wizard is complete, click Finish.

16. Expand Policies node below NPS (Local) and then click the Connection Request Policies node. Take a screen shot of the Network Policy Server window by pressing Alt+Prt Scr and then paste it into your Lab12_worksheet file in the page provided by pressing Ctrl+V.

End of exercise. Leave the Network Policy Server console open for the next exercise.

Exercise 12.3	Managing RADIUS Templates
Overview	During this exercise, you use RADIUS templates to simplify the deployment of RADIUS in the future..
Mindset	RADIUS templates simplify the configuration of RADIUS servers by creating RADIUS configuration elements such as IP filters or Shared Secrets, and reuse them on local NPS servers. The templates can also be exported to a file and then imported into another NPS server
Completion time	10 minutes

1. On RWDC01, using Network Policy Server console, double-click Templates Management.

2. Right-click Shared Secrets and choose New. The New RADIUS Shared Secret Template opens.

3. In the Template name text box, type Shared Secret Template.

4. In the Shared secret and Confirm shared secret text boxes, type **Pa$$w0rd** and then click OK.

Question 6	*During the lab exercises, you have been using Pa$$w0rd for domain admins and user logins. In reality, should you use the same password for templates? If you are or are not, explain why?*

5. Under RADIUS Clients and Servers, click RADIUS Clients.

6. In the RADIUS Clients pane, double-click Server01. The Server01 Properties dialog box opens.

7. In the Shared Secret section, in the drop-down arrow list, select the Shared Secret Template and then click OK.

8. Right-click Templates Management and choose Export Templates to a File.

9. In the File Name text box, type **Templates** and then click Save.

10. Right-click Templates Management and choose Import Templates from a File.

11. Scroll down and click Templates.xml and then click Open.

End of exercise. Leave the Network Policy Server console open for the next exercise.

Exercise 12.4	Configuring RADIUS Accounting
Overview	Although RADIUS is used for central authentication, it can also be used for accounting. During this exercise, you configure RADIUS accounting.
Mindset	The two uses of RADIUS accounting are to track network usage for auditing and billing purposes
Completion time	5 minutes

1. On RWDC01, using the Network Policy Server console, on the NPS (Local) tree, click Accounting.

2. In the Accounting section, click Configure Accounting. When the Accounting Configuration Wizard starts, click Next.

3. On the Select Accounting Options page, click Log to a text file on the local computer and then click Next.

4. On the Configure Local File Logging page, click Next.

Question 7	Where are the logs stored?

5. Take a screen shot of the Summary page by pressing Alt+Prt Scr and then paste it into your Lab12_worksheet file in the page provided by pressing Ctrl+V.

6. Click Next.

7. On the Conclusion page, click Close.

End of exercise.

LAB REVIEW QUESTIONS

Completion time	10 minutes

1. In Exercise 12.1, what program is used as the RADIUS server in Microsoft Windows servers?

2. In Exercise 12.2, what is a VPN server or wireless access point from the point-of-view of the NPS server?

3. In Exercise 12.2, when a user, using his or her laptop, connects to a VPN server, what is the laptop considered when discussing RADIUS?

4. In Exercise 12.3, if you decide to deploy several RADIUS servers, what can you use to help manage the deployment and configuration of servers?

5. In Exercise 12.4, what are the two methods used to record events used in RADIUS accounting?

Lab Challenge	Add Workstation Authentication Certificates to All Workstations
Overview	To complete this challenge, you will demonstrate how to add workstation authentication certificates to all workstations by writing the steps to complete the tasks described in the scenerio.
Mindset	You decide to use RADIUS for your organization. To ensure a secure environment, you decide to use digital certificates. How would you automatically add workstation authentication certificates to all client computers within your organization?
Completion time	15 minutes

Write out the steps you performed to complete the challenge.

End of lab.

LAB 13
CONFIGURING NPS POLICIES

THIS LAB CONTAINS THE FOLLOWING EXERCISES AND ACTIVITIES:

Exercise 13.1   Creating and Configuring Connection Request Policies

Exercise 13.2   Creating and Configuring Network Policies

Exercise 13.3   Exporting and Importing the NPS Configuration

Lab Challenge   Processing Network Policies

BEFORE YOU BEGIN

The lab environment consists of student workstations connected to a local area network, along with a server that functions as the domain controller for a domain called *contoso.com*. The computers required for this lab are listed in Table 13-1.

Table 13-1
Computers Required for Lab 13

Computer	Operating System	Computer Name
Server (VM 1)	Windows Server 2012 R2	RWDC01

In addition to the computers, you also require the software listed in Table 13-2 to complete Lab 13.

Table 13-2
Software Required for Lab 13

Software	Location
Lab 13 student worksheet	Lab13_worksheet.docx (provided by instructor)

Working with Lab Worksheets

Each lab in this manual requires that you answer questions, take screen shots, and perform other activities that you will document in a worksheet named for the lab, such as Lab13_worksheet.docx. You will find these worksheets on the book companion site. It is recommended that you use a USB flash drive to store your worksheets, so you can submit them to your instructor for review. As you perform the exercises in each lab, open the appropriate worksheet file using Word, fill in the required information, and save the file to your flash drive.

After completing this lab, you will be able to:

- Create and Configure connection request policies

- Create and Configure network policies

- Import and export the NPS configuration

- Understand how network policies are processed

Estimated lab time: 55 minutes

Exercise 13.1	Creating and Configuring Connection Request Policies
Overview	In this exercise, you start using NPS policies, specifically the Connection Request Policies.
Mindset	Connection request policies are used to establish sets of connections and settings that RADIUS servers perform when authenticating, authorizing, and accounting connection requests through the RADIUS clients.
Completion time	15 minutes

1. Log in to RWDC01 as the Contoso\administrator user account and the Pa$$w0rd password. The Server Manager console opens.

2. On Server Manager, click Tools > Network Policy Server. The Network Policy Server console opens.

3. Double-click Policies in the NPS (Local) tree.

Question 1	What does the default connection request policy do?

4. Right-click Connection Request Policies and choose New. The New Connection Request Policy wizard starts.

5. In the Policy name text box, type **Connection Request Policy 1** in the Policy name text box.

6. Under Type of network access server, select Remote Access Server (VPN-Dial up) and then click Next.

7. On the Specify Conditions page, click Add.

8. When the Select condition dialog box opens, click Tunnel Type and then click Add.

9. When the Tunnel Type dialog box opens, click IP Encapsulating Security Payload in the Tunnel-mode (ESP), Layer Two Tunneling Protocol (L2TP), and Secure Socket Tunneling Protocol (SSTP). Click OK.

10. Click Add, click Day and Time Restrictions, and then click Add again.

11. In the Day and time restrictions dialog box, click Monday through Friday, 8 AM to 5 PM, and click Permitted. A blue box should appear as shown in Figure 13-1. Click OK.

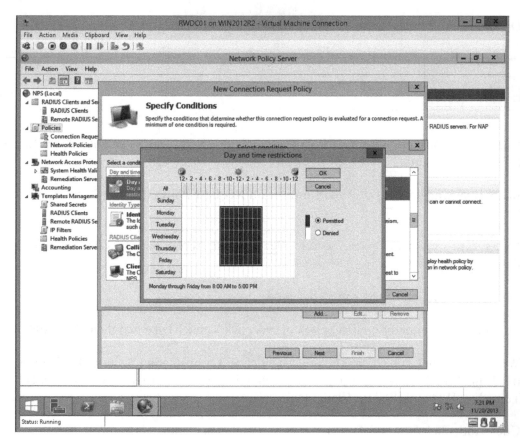

Figure 13-1
Restricting access by day and time

12. Back on the Specify Conditions page, click Next.

13. On the Specify Connection Request Forwarding page, click Next.

14. On the Specify Authentication Methods page, click Next.

15. On the Configure Settings page, click Next.

16. Take a screen shot of the Completing Connection Request Policy Wizard by pressing Alt+Prt Scr and then paste it into your Lab13_worksheet file in the page provided by pressing Ctrl+V.

17. On the Completing Connection Request Policy Wizard page, click Finish. When created, the Connection Policy is listed in the Network Policies pane.

End of exercise. Leave the Network Policy Server console open for the next exercise.

Exercise 13.2	Creating and Configuring Network Policies
Overview	During this exercise, you continue to use NPS policies by creating and configuring Network Policies.
Mindset	Network policies establish sets of conditions, constraints, and settings that specify who is authorized to connect to the network and the circumstances under which the user can or cannot connect.
Completion time	10 minutes

1. On RWDC01, using the Network Policy Server, right-click Network Policies and choose New. The New Network Policy wizard opens as shown in Figure 13-2.

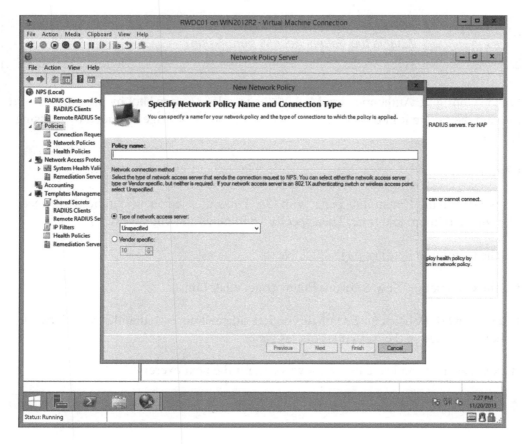

Figure 13-2
Creating a new network policy

2. In the Policy name text box, type **Network Policy 1** in the Policy name text box.

3. For the type of network access server, select Remote Access Server (VPN-Dial up) and then click Next.

Question 2	*What are the three components that make up a NPS network policy?*

4. On the Specify Conditions page, click Add.

5. When the Select condition dialog box opens, click Windows Groups and then click Add.

6. Click Add Groups. In the Enter the object name to select text box, type **domain guests** and then click OK. Click OK to close the Windows Groups dialog box. Click Next.

7. On the Specify Access Permission page, answer the following question, and then click Next.

Question 3	*What is the default access permission?*

8. On the Configure Authentication Methods page, take a screen shot by pressing Alt+Prt Scr and then paste it into your Lab13_worksheet file in the page provided by pressing Ctrl+V.

9. Click Next.

10. On the Configure Constraints page, with Idle Timeout selected, select the Disconnect after the maximum idle time. Then specify 15 minutes and click Next.

11. On the Configure Settings page, click Next.

12. On the Completing New Network Policy page, click Finish.

13. Click Network Policies under Policies on left side and observe that the new Network Policy 1 is listed in the Network Policies pane.

End of exercise. You can leave the windows open for the next exercise.

Exercise 13.3	Exporting and Importing the NPS Configuration
Overview	In the previous lab, you created and used NPS templates to help configure RADIUS. During this lesson, you export the configuration for the NPS server to an XML file and then import the configuration back into the system.
Mindset	You can export the entire NPS configuration, including RADIUS clients and servers, network policy, connection request policy, registry, and logging configuration, from one NPS server for import on another NPS server by using the netsh command.
Completion time	10 minutes

1. On RWDC01, open a Command Prompt (Admin) window.

2. Type **netsh** and then press Enter.

3. At the netsh prompt, type **nps** and then press Enter.

4. At the netsh nps prompt, type **export filename="C:\Bak.xml" exportPSK=YES** and then press Enter.

Question 4	*What does the warning say?*

5. At the command prompt, type **exit** and then press Enter.

6. To import back in, type **netsh nps import filename="C:\Bak.xml"** and then press Enter. A message appears indicating whether the import from the XML file was successful.

7. Take a screen shot of the Command Prompt window by pressing Alt+Prt Scr and then paste it into your Lab13_worksheet file in the page provided by pressing Ctrl+V.

8. When the import is complete, close the Administrator: Command Prompt and then close the Network Policy console.

End of exercise.

LAB REVIEW QUESTIONS

Completion time	10 minutes

1. In Exercise 13.1, if you want to configure a RADIUS proxy and forward connection requests to another NPS or RADIUS server, what must you do?

2. In Exercise 13.1, when you create a connection request policy, what parameters do you configure?

3. In Exercise 13.2, if you had multiple network policies, why does order matter?

4. In Exercise 13.2, where would you configure multilink and bandwidth allocation?

Lab Challenge	Processing Network Policies
Overview	To complete this challenge, you will describe how network policies are processed by writing the high-level steps of processing network policies.
Mindset	During this lab, you started to use NPS policies, specifically the Connection Request policies and Network Policies. Although the connection request policy specified settings for the RADIUS server, the network policy will allow or disallow the remote access.
Completion time	10 minutes

What are the steps used when processing network policies?

End of lab.

LAB 14
CONFIGURING NETWORK ACCESS PROTECTION (NAP)

THIS LAB CONTAINS THE FOLLOWING EXERCISES AND ACTIVITIES:

Exercise 14.1   Installing Health Registration Authority Role on an NPS Server

Exercise 14.2   Configuring NAP Enforcement for DHCP

Exercise 14.3   Configuring SHV and Health Policies

Lab Challenge   Configuring Clients for NAP

BEFORE YOU BEGIN

The lab environment consists of student workstations connected to a local area network, along with a server that functions as the domain controller for a domain called *contoso.com*. The computers required for this lab are listed in Table 14-1.

Table 14-1
Computers Required for Lab 14

Computer	Operating System	Computer Name
Server (VM 1)	Windows Server 2012 R2	RWDC01
Server (VM 2)	Windows Server 2012 R2	Server01

In addition to the computers, you also require the software listed in Table 14-2 to complete Lab 14.

Table 14-2
Software Required for Lab 14

Software	Location
Lab 14 student worksheet	Lab14_worksheet.docx (provided by instructor)

Working with Lab Worksheets

Each lab in this manual requires that you answer questions, take screen shots, and perform other activities that you will document in a worksheet named for the lab, such as Lab14_worksheet.docx. You will find these worksheets on the book companion site. It is recommended that you use a USB flash drive to store your worksheets, so you can submit them to your instructor for review. As you perform the exercises in each lab, open the appropriate worksheet file using Word, fill in the required information, and save the file to your flash drive.

After completing this lab, you will be able to:

■ Install Health Registration Authority role on an NPS server

■ Install and configure NAP Enforcement using DHCP

■ Configure System Health Validators (SHVs)

■ Configure health policies

■ Configure NAP client settings

Estimated lab time: 60 minutes

Exercise 14.1	Installing Health Registration Authority Role on an NPS Server
Overview	Network Access Protection (NAP), which is used to control who can access a network based on the security health of a client, is one of the more complicated installations during this course. Before you can configure NAP, you must add the Health Registration Authority role to the current NPS installation on RWDC01 so that it can monitor the connections on the NPS server.
Mindset	Network Access Protection (NAP) is Microsoft's software for controlling network access for computers based on the health of the host including whether the computer has a firewall, whether the computer has a current anti-virus or anti-spyware package or whether the computer has the newest updates. NAP is used to ensure that the individual computers are secure before connecting to the network.
Completion time	10 minutes

1. Log in to RWDC01 as the Contoso\administrator user account and the Pa$$w0rd password. The Server Manager console opens.

2. On Server Manager, click Manage > Add Roles and Features. The Add Roles and Feature Wizard opens.

Question 1	To use NAP with DHCP, which server do you need to install NPS on?

3. On the Before you begin page, click Next.

4. Select Role-based or feature-based installation and then click Next.

5. On the Select destination server page, click Next.

6. On the Select server roles page, expand Network Policy and Access Services (1 of 3 Installed), and then click to select Health Registration Authority.

7. When you are prompted to add features that are required for Health Registration Authority, click Add Features.

8. On the Select server roles page, click Next.

9. On the Select features page, click Next.

10. On the Network Policy and Access Services page, click Next.

11. Click Use the local CA to issue health certificates for this HRA server. Click Next.

12. On the Authentication Requirements page, select the Yes, require requestors to be authenticated as members of a domain. (recommended). Click Next.

13. On the Server Authentication Certificate page, make sure Choose an existing certificate for SSL encryption (recommended) is selected. Click to highlight RWDC01.contoso.com and then click Next.

14. On the Confirm installation selection page, click Install.

15. When the installation is complete, take a screen shot of the Installation progress page by pressing Alt+Prt Scr and then paste it into your Lab14_worksheet file in the page provided by pressing Ctrl+V.

16. Click Close.

End of exercise.

Exercise 14.2	Configuring NAP Enforcement for DHCP
Overview	During this exercise, you configure NAP enforcement for DHCP, specify the remediation servers, and enable NAP for a DHCP scope.
Mindset	The DHCP enforcement method uses DHCP configuration information to ensure that NAP clients remain in compliance. If a computer is out of compliance, NAP provides a Dynamic Host Configuration Protocol (DHCP) configuration that limits a user's access to the network until the computer is compliant. DHCP enforcement is considered the weakest form of NAP enforcement because it can be bypassed with the client computer using static IP addresses.
Completion time	20 minutes

1. On RWDC01, right-click the Start button and choose Command Prompt (Admin).

2. At the command prompt, execute the **napclcfg.msc** command. The NAP Client Configuration console opens, as shown in Figure 14-1.

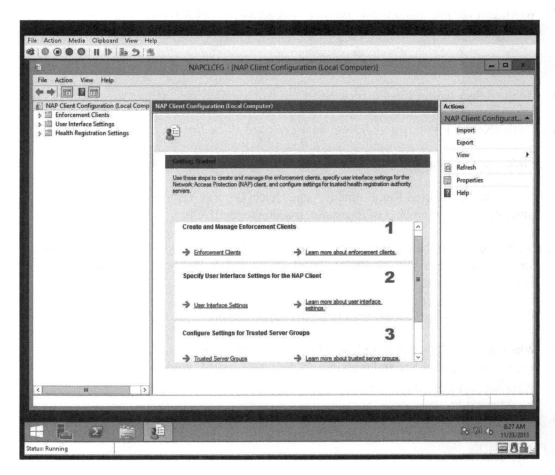

Figure 14-1
Opening the NAP Client Configuration console

3. In the left pane, click Enforcement Clients.

4. In the center pane, double-click DHCP Quarantine Enforcement Client to open the DHCP Quarantine Enforcement Client Properties dialog box.

5. Select the Enable this enforcement client option. Click OK to close the DHCP Quarantine Enforcement Client Properties dialog box.

6. Take a screen shot of the NAP Client Configuration window by pressing Alt+Prt Scr and then paste it into your Lab14_worksheet file in the page provided by pressing Ctrl+V.

7. Close the NAP Client Configuration Client console.

8. At the command prompt, execute the **services.msc** command.

9. Scroll down and find the Network Access Protection Agent. Then double-click the Network Access Protection Agent service to open the Network Access Protection Agent Properties dialog box.

10. Change the Startup type to Automatic.

11. Take a screen shot of the Network Access Protection Agent Properties dialog box by pressing Alt+Prt Scr and then paste it into your Lab14_worksheet file in the page provided by pressing Ctrl+V.

12. Click the Start button.

13. After the service is started, click OK to close the Network Access Protection Agent Properties dialog box.

14. Close the Services console and close the command prompt.

15. Using Server Manager, click Tools > Network Policy Server. The Network Policy Server console opens.

16. In the main pane, click the Configure NAP link to start the Configure NAP Wizard.

17. When the Select Network Connection Method For Use with NAP wizard opens, select the Dynamic Host Configuration Protocol (DHCP) for the network connection method from the drop-down list. Click Next.

18. On the Specify NAP Enforcement Servers Running DHCP Server page, highlight Server01 and then click Next.

19. On the Specify DHCP Scopes page, click the Add button to open the MS-Server Class page. Type **NAP DHCP** in the text box and then click OK. On the Specify DHCP Scopes page, click Next.

20. On the Configure Machine Groups page, click the Add button to open the Select Group dialog box. In the Enter the object name to select text box, type **domain computers** and then click OK. Click Next.

21. On the Specify a NAP Remediation Server Group and URL page, click New Group. In the Group Name text box, type **Remediation Servers**.

Question 2	*What remediation servers should you include?*

22. Click the Add button. In the Friendly name text box, type **Server01**. For the IP address or DNS name, type **Server01.contoso.com** and then click Resolve. Click OK to close the Add New Server dialog box and then click OK to close the New Remediation Server Group dialog box. Click Next.

23. On the Define NAP Health Policy page, click Next.

24. Take a screen shot of the Completing NAP Enforcement Policy and RADIUS Client Configuration page by pressing Alt+Prt Scr and then paste it into your Lab14_worksheet file in the page provided by pressing Ctrl+V.

25. On the Completing NAP Enforcement Policy and RADIUS Client Configuration page, click Finish.

26. Using Server Manager, click Tools > DHCP. The DHCP console opens.

27. Expand the server node and expand the IPv4 node.

28. Click Scope [192.168.1.0]. Then right-click Scope [192.168.1.0] and choose Properties. A Scope Properties dialog box opens.

29. Click the Network Access Protection tab.

30. Click Enable for this scope.

31. Click OK to close the Scope [192.168.1.0] Main Scope Properties dialog box.

32. Close DHCP console.

End of exercise. Leave the Network Policy Server window open for the next exercise.

Exercise 14.3	Configuring SHV and Health Policies
Overview	During this exercise, to enforce NAP, you configure System Health Validator and Health Policies.
Mindset	The System Health Agents (SHAs) and System Health Validators (SHVs) provide health-state status and validation. Windows 8 includes a Windows Security Health Validator SHA that monitors the Windows Security Center settings. Windows Server 2012 includes a corresponding Windows Security Health Validator SHV.
Completion time	10 minutes

1. On RWDC01, click the Network Policy Server icon in the task bar, if needed.

2. Expand Network Access Protection, expand System Health Validators, expand Windows Security Health Validator, and then click Windows Security Health Validator.

3. Click the Settings link and then double-click Default Configuration. The Windows Security Health Validator dialog box opens as shown in Figure 14-2.

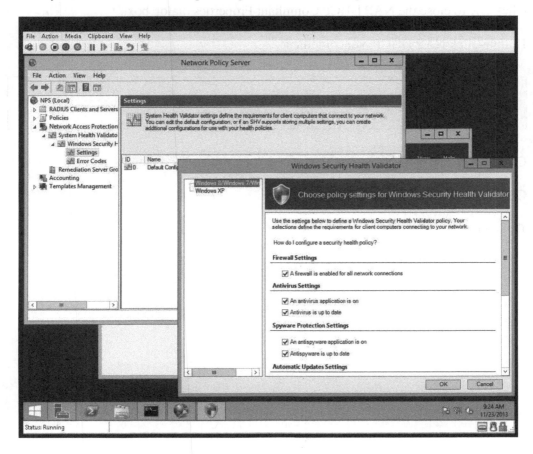

Figure 14-2
Configuring the Windows Security Health Validator

Question 3	Which options are already selected for the Windows Security Health Validator?

4. Click OK to close the Windows Security Health Validator.

5. In the NPS console, under Policies, click Health Policies.

6. Double-click NAP DHCP Compliant.

Question 4	Which Windows Security Health Validator is configured?

Question 5	What is the Client SHV checks configured as?

7. Click OK to close the NAP DHCP Compliant Properties dialog box.

8. Double-click NAP DHCP Noncompliant.

Question 6	What is the Client SHV checks configured as?

9. Click OK to close the NAP DHCP Noncompliant Properties dialog box.

10. Close Network Policy Server console.

End of exercise.

LAB REVIEW QUESTIONS

Completion time	10 minutes

1. In Exercise 14.1, you installed support for the Health Registration Authority. What does the Health Registration Authority do?

2. In Exercise 14.2, what command opened the NAP Client Configuration console?

3. In Exercise 14.2, what allows a computer to get Windows update so that it can be compliant when using NAP?

4. In Exercise 14.3, when using NAP, what defines the requirements for client computers that connect to the network?

Lab Challenge	Configuring Clients for NAP
Overview	To complete this challenge, you will explain how to configure clients for NAP by writing the high level steps to complete the tasks described in the scenerio.
Mindset	So far, you have configured NAP on the servers. You now need to configure NAP for the clients. Explain how to enable Security Center and to automatically start Network Access Protection Agent services.
Completion time	10 minutes

Write out the steps you performed to complete the challenge.

End of lab.

LAB 15
CONFIGURING SERVER AUTHENTICATION

THIS LAB CONTAINS THE FOLLOWING EXERCISES AND ACTIVITIES: _ _ _ _ _

Exercise 15.1	Creating a Service Account
Exercise 15.2	Creating a Managed Service Account
Exercise 15.3	Using Virtual Accounts
Exercise 15.4	Configuring Kerberos and Kerberos Delegation
Lab Challenge	Configuring Kerberos with the setspn Command

BEFORE YOU BEGIN

The lab environment consists of student workstations connected to a local area network, along with a server that functions as the domain controller for a domain called *contoso.com*. The computers required for this lab are listed in Table 15-1.

Table 15-1
Computers Required for Lab 15

Computer	Operating System	Computer Name
Server (VM 1)	Windows Server 2012 R2	RWDC01
Server (VM 2)	Windows Server 2012 R2	Server01

In addition to the computers, you also require the software listed in Table 15-2 to complete Lab 15.

Table 15-2
Software Required for Lab 15

Software	Location
Lab 15 student worksheet	Lab15_worksheet.docx (provided by instructor)

Working with Lab Worksheets

Each lab in this manual requires that you answer questions, take screen shots, and perform other activities that you will document in a worksheet named for the lab, such as Lab15_worksheet.docx. You will find these worksheets on the book companion site. It is recommended that you use a USB flash drive to store your worksheets, so you can submit them to your instructor for review. As you perform the exercises in each lab, open the appropriate worksheet file using Word, fill in the required information, and save the file to your flash drive.

After completing this lab, you will be able to:

- Create a service account

- Create a Group Service Account

- Configure Kerberos and Kerberos Delegation

Estimated lab time: 70 minutes

Exercise 15.1	Creating a Service Account
Overview	In this exercise, you create a traditional service account.
Mindset	A service account is an account under which an operating system, process, or service runs. A service account can allow the application or service specific rights and permissions to function properly while minimizing the permissions required for the users using the application server.
Completion time	10 minutes

1. Log on to RWDC01 as the Contoso\administrator user account with the Pa$$w0rd password. The Server Manager console opens.

2. On Server Manager, click Tools > Active Directory Users and Computers.

3. In the console tree, expand contoso.com, if needed.

4. Right-click contoso.com and choose New > Organizational Unit. The New Object – Organizational Unit dialog box opens.

5. In the Name text box, type Service Accounts and then click OK.

6. Right-click the Service Accounts organizational unit and choose New > User. The New Object – User Wizard starts.

7. In the First name text box, type **App1**. In the Last name text box, type **Service**. In the User logon name text box, type **App1Service**. Click Next.

    The password options appear.

8. In the Password and Confirm password dialog boxes, type **Pa$$w0rd**. Select the Password never expires option. When a dialog box opens, indicating that the password should never expire and that the user will not be required to change the password at next logon, click OK.

9. Click Next.

10. Click Finish to complete creating a service account.

11. Take a screen shot of the Active Directory Users and Computers page showing the Service Accounts OU by pressing Alt+Prt+ Scr and then paste it into your Lab15_worksheet file in the page provided by pressing Ctrl+V.

Question 1	What is the disadvantage of using a traditional service account?

End of exercise. Leave any windows open for the next exercise.

Exercise 15.2	Creating a Managed Service Account
Overview	During this exercise, you create and deploy a Managed Service Account (MSA).
Mindset	Rather than manually changing the account password and the password for the service or application, you can use the Managed Service Account (MSA) where the password will automatically change on a regular basis.
Completion time	25 minutes

1. On RWDC01, using Server Manager, click Tools > Active Directory Users and Computers, if needed.

2. In Active Directory Users and Computers, right-click the Computers container and choose New > Group. For the Group name, type **ServerGroup** and click OK.

3. In the Computers container, right-click ServerGroup and then click Properties.

4. When the Properties dialog box opens, click the Members tab.

5. Click Add. In the text box, type **Server01.**

6. Click Object Types, select Computers, and then click OK twice.

7. Click OK to close the ServerGroup Properties dialog box.

8. On RWDC01, using Server Manager, click Tools > Active Directory Module for Windows PowerShell. The Active Directory Module for Windows Powershell opens.

9. To create a key distribution services root key for the domain, execute the following command in PowerShell:

   ```
   Add-KDSRootKey -EffectiveTime ((Get-Date).AddHours(-10))
   ```

10. To create an Active Directory AD service account, execute the following command:

    ```
    New-ADServiceAccount -Name App2Service -DNSHostname
    rwdc01.contoso.com
    -PrincipalsAllowedToRetrieveManagedPassword ServerGroup
    ```

11. Answer Question 2 below.

12. Take a screen shot of the Active Directory Users and Computers showing the Managed Service Account OU by pressing Alt+Prt Scr and then paste it into your Lab15_worksheet file in the page provided by pressing Ctrl+V.

Question 2	In which OU was the account created?

13. To associate an MSA to a computer account, execute the following command in Windows PowerShell:

    ```
    Add-ADComputerServiceAccount -identity server01
    -ServiceAccount App2Service
    ```

14. Log in to Server01 as the Contoso\administrator user account and the Pa$$w0rd password. The Server Manager console opens.

15. Click Manage > Add Roles and Features.

16. When the Add Roles and Features Wizard opens, click Next.

17. On the Select installation type page, click Next.

18. On the Select destination server page, click Next.

19. Click Active Directory Domain Services. When you are prompted to add features, click Add Features and then click Next.

20. On the Select features page, click Next.

21. On the Active Directory Domain Services page, click Next.

22. On the Confirm installation selections page, click Install.

23. When the installation is complete, click Close.

24. On Server01, with Server Manager, click Tools > Active Directory Module for Windows PowerShell.

25. When Windows PowerShell starts, execute the following command to add the computer account to Server01:

```
Add-ADComputerserviceaccount -Identity Server01
-ServiceAccount App2Service
```

26. On Server01, with Server Manager, open the Tools menu and click Services. The Services console opens.

27. Double-click the SNMP Trap service. The SNMP Trap Properties dialog box opens.

28. Click the Log On tab.

29. Select This account option and then type **contoso\app2service$**.

Question 3	*Why is the $ used?*

30. Clear the password in the Password and Confirm password text boxes.

31. Click OK.

32. When a message indicates that the account has been granted the Log On As Service, click OK.

33. If a message indicates that the new logon name will not take effect until you stop and restart the service, click OK.

End of exercise. Leave the windows open for the next exercise.

Exercise 15.3	Using Virtual Accounts
Overview	In this exercise, you will create a virtual account that will be assigned to the print service.
Mindset	A virtual account is an account that emulates a Network Service account that has the name NT Service\servicename. The virtual account has simplified service administration including automatic password management, and simplified service principal name (SPN) management.
Completion time	10 minutes

1. If necessary, log on to Server01 as contoso\administrator with the Pa$$w0rd password.

2. If necessary, using Server Manager, click Tools > Services.

3. Double-click the SNMP Trap service. The SNMP Trap Properties dialog box opens.

Question 4	What is the service name for Print Spooler?

4. Click the Log on tab.

5. Select This account and, in the This account text box, type **NT Service\SNMPTrap**.

6. For the Password text box and the Confirm Password text box, make sure that the text boxes are empty.

7. Click OK to close the SNMP Trap Properties dialog box.

8. If the Services dialog box displays, indicating that the new logon name will not take effect until you stop and restart the service, click OK.

9. Right-click the service and choose Restart.

End of Exercise. Close the Services console and close the Windows PowerShell command box.

Exercise 15.4	Configuring Kerberos and Kerberos Delegation
Overview	In this exercise, you create a service principal name (SPN) for an account and configure Kerberos Delegation.
Mindset	A service principal name is the name by which a client uniquely identifies an instance of a service. The client locates the service based on the SPN, which consists of three components: The service class, such as HTTP (which includes both the HTTP and HTTPS protocols) or SQLService; the host name; and the port (if port 80 is not being used).
Completion time	10 minutes

Question 5	*Which component in Active Directory performs authentication for Kerberos?*

1. On RWDC01, using Server Manager, click Tools > ADSI Edit. The ADSI Edit console opens.

2. Right-click ADSI Edit in the console tree and choose Connect To. When the Connection Settings dialog displays, click OK.

3. Double-click Default Naming Context in the console tree, expand DC=contoso, DC=com and then click OU=Service Account.

4. In the Details pane, right-click the CN=App1 Service and choose Properties. The CN=App1 Service Properties dialog box opens as shown in Figure 15-1.

Figure 15-1
Editing the properties of a user

5. In the Attributes list, double-click servicePrincipalName to display the Multi-valued String Editor dialog box.

6. In the Value to add field, type **http/portal.contoso.com:443** and then click Add.

7. Click OK twice.

8. Using Server Manager, click Tools > Active Directory Users and Computers.

9. Navigate to and click the Service Accounts organizational unit.

10. Right-click App1 Service and choose Properties. The Properties dialog box opens.

11. Click the Delegation tab.

12. To allow this account to be delegated for a service, click Trust this user for delegation to any service (Kerberos only).

13. Click OK to close the Properties dialog box.

LAB REVIEW QUESTIONS

Completion time	10 minutes

1. In Exercise 15.2, what are the minimum requirements for Managed Service Accounts?

2. In Exercise 15.2, when using the PrincipalsAllowedToRetrieveManagedPassword option, what kind of objects can you specify?

3. In Exercise 15.2, what do you use to create a Managed Service Account?

4. In Exercise 15.3, what was used to define an SPN for an account?

Lab Challenge	Configuring Kerberos with the setspn Command
Overview	To complete this challenge, you will demonstrate how to configure Kerberos with the setspn command by writing the command and taking a screen shot of the setspn command prompt window.
Mindset	You need to configure an SPN for an account. You decide that you want to create the SPN using the command prompt. Which command should be used to configure the SPN in the same way that you did in Exercise 15.4?
Completion time	5 minutes

Write the command that you used, and then take a screen shot of the netsh command prompt window by pressing Alt+Prt Scr and then paste it into your Lab15_worksheet file in the page provided by pressing Ctrl+V.

End of lab.

LAB 16
CONFIGURING DOMAIN CONTROLLERS

THIS LAB CONTAINS THE FOLLOWING EXERCISES AND ACTIVITIES:

Exercise 16.1   Promoting Server01 to a Domain Controller

Exercise 16.2   Configuring Universal Group Membership Caching

Exercise 16.3   Moving Operations Masters

Exercise 16.4   Seizing Operations Masters

Exercise 16.5   Creating an RODC

Lab Challenge   Cloning a Domain Controller

BEFORE YOU BEGIN

The lab environment consists of student workstations connected to a local area network, along with a server that functions as the domain controller for a domain called *contoso.com*. The computers required for this lab are listed in Table 16-1.

Table 16-1
Computers Required for Lab 16

Computer	Operating System	Computer Name
Server (VM 1)	Windows Server 2012 R2	RWDC01
Server (VM 2)	Windows Server 2012 R2	Server01
Server (VM 3)	Windows Server 2012 R2	Server02

In addition to the computers, you also require the software listed in Table 16-2 to complete Lab 16.

Table 16-2
Software Required for Lab 16

Software	Location
Lab 16 student worksheet	Lab16_worksheet.docx (provided by instructor)

Working with Lab Worksheets

Each lab in this manual requires that you answer questions, shoot screen shots, and perform other activities that you will document in a worksheet named for the lab, such as Lab16_worksheet.docx. You will find these worksheets on the book companion site. It is recommended that you use a USB flash drive to store your worksheets, so you can submit them to your instructor for review. As you perform the exercises in each lab, open the appropriate worksheet file using Word, fill in the required information, and save the file to your flash drive.

After completing this lab, you will be able to:

■ Configure universal group membership caching (UGMC)

■ Transfer and seize operations masters

■ Install and configure a Read-Only Domain Controller

■ Clone a Domain Controller

Estimated lab time: 95 minutes

Exercise 16.1	Promoting Server01 to a Domain Controller
Overview	During this exercise, you promote Server01 to a domain controller.
Mindset	A domain controller is a Windows server that stores a replica of the account and security information for the domain and defines the domain boundaries. To make a computer running Windows Server 2012 a domain controller, you must install the AD DS and execute dcpromo from Server Manager.
Completion time	10 minutes

1. Log in to Server01 as the Contoso\administrator user account with the Pa$$w0rd password. The Server Manager console opens.

2. Click the Yellow triangle with the black exclamation point (!) and click Promote this server to a domain controller.

3. When the Deployment Configuration page opens, click Next.

4. On the Domain Controller Options page, type **Pa$$w0rd** in the Password and Confirm password text boxes and click Next.

5. On the DNS Options page, click Next.

6. On the Additional Options page, click Next.

7. On the Paths page, click Next.

8. On the Review Options page, click Next.

9. After the prerequisites are checked, click Install.

10. When the promotion is done, the system restarts automatically.

End of exercise. You can leave the windows open for the next exercise.

Exercise 16.2	Configuring Universal Group Membership Caching
Overview	In this exercise, you enable Universal Group Membership Caching so that your network can become more fault tolerant.
Mindset	Users need to be able to access universal groups to log in. Therefore, to log in, they will either need to access the global catalogs or you will need to have enabled universal group membership caching (UGMC).
Completion time	5 minutes

1. Log in to RWDC01 as the Contoso\administrator user account with the Pa$$w0rd password. The Server Manager console opens.

2. On Server Manager, click Tools > Active Directory Sites and Services. The Active Directory Sites and Services console opens.

Question 1	*What program is used to enable or disable global catalogs?*

3. Expand Sites, and click Default-First-Site-Name.

4. Right-click NTDS Site Settings and choose Properties. The NTDS Site Settings Properties dialog box opens as shown in Figure 16-1.

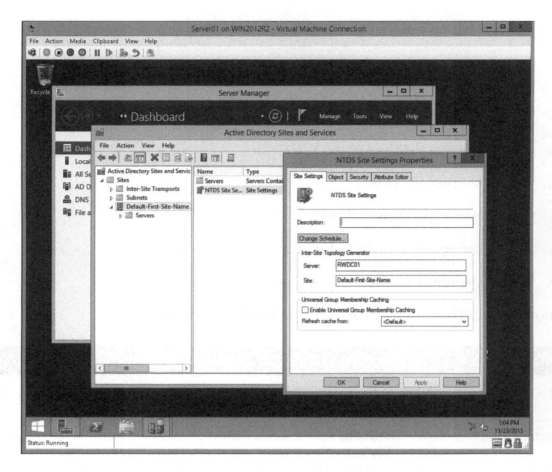

Figure 16-1
Modifying site settings

5. Select the Enable Universal Group Membership Caching option.

6. Click OK to close the NTDS Settings Properties dialog box.

7. Close Active Directory Sites and Services.

End of exercise.

Exercise 16.3	Moving Operations Master
Overview	During this exercise, you transfer the Operations Masters to another domain controller.
Mindset	If you know that you will be performing maintenance, which will cause the operations masters to be unavailable, you should move them to other domain controllers that will be available during the maintenance period. Although the operations masters are not available, users might have trouble with recently changed passwords. In addition, you will not be able to perform certain tasks such as create new domains, perform time synchronization, and other functions that require the operations masters.
Completion time	20 minutes

1. Log in to Server01 as the Contoso\administrator user account with the Pa$$w0rd password. The Server Manager console opens.

2. On Server Manager, click Tools > Active Directory Users and Computers. The Active Directory Users and Computers console opens.

3. Right-click contoso.com and choose Change Domain Controller. Click Server01.contoso.com and click OK.

4. Right-click contoso.com and choose Operations Masters. The Operations Masters dialog box opens as shown in Figure 16-2.

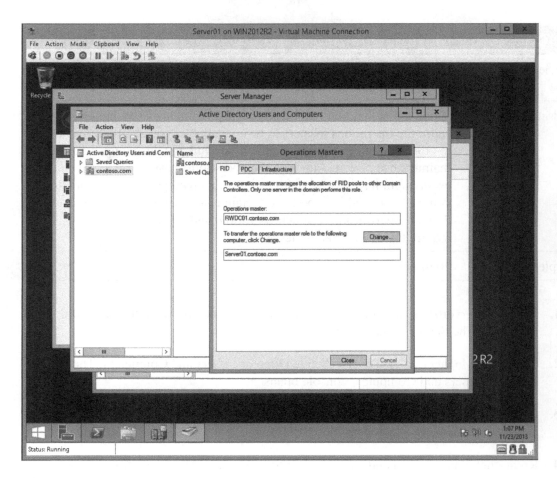

Figure 16-2
Viewing the current domain-level operations masters

5. To transfer the RID from RWDC01 to Server01, click Change on the RID tab. When you are prompted to confirm that you are sure, click Yes. When the Operations Master role is transferred, click OK.

6. Click the PDC tab. Transfer the PDC Emulator to Server01.

Question 2	Which Operations Master acts as the master time server and is considered authoritative for account passwords?

7. Click the Infrastructure tab. Transfer the Infrastructure to Server01.

8. Close the Operations Masters dialog box.

9. Close the Active Directory Users and Computers console.

10. On Server01, using Server Manager, click Tools > Active Directory Domains and Trusts. The Active Domains and Trusts console opens.

11. Right-click Active Directory Domains and Trusts and choose Change Active Directory Domain Controller. Click Server01.contoso.com. Click OK.

12. Right-click Active Directory Domains and Trusts and choose Operations Master. The Operations Master dialog box showing current Domain naming operations master opens.

13. Take a screen shot of the Operations Master window by pressing Alt+Prt Scr and then paste it into your Lab16_worksheet file in the page provided by pressing Ctrl+V.

14. To transfer the Operations Master, click Change. When you are prompted to confirm this action, click Yes and then click OK.

15. Click Close to close the Operations Master dialog box.

16. Close the Active Directory Domains and Trusts console.

17. Right-click the start button and choose Command Prompt (Admin). The command prompt opens.

18. At the command prompt, execute the following command so that you can use the Schema Management console.

```
Regsvr32 schmmgmt.dll
```

19. When the schmmgmt.dll is registered, click OK.

20. At the command prompt, execute the mmc command. The MMC console opens.

21. Click File > Add/Remove Snap-in. The Add or Remove Snap-ins dialog box opens.

22. Select Active Directory Schema and click Add. Then click OK to close the Add/Remove Snap-ins dialog box.

23. Right-click Active Directory Schema and choose Change Active Directory Domain Controller. Click Server01.contoso.com and click OK. When a warning displays, click OK.

24. Right-click Active Directory Schema (Server01.contoso.com) and choose Operations Master. The Change Schema Master dialog box opens.

25. To transfer the Schema Master to Server01, click Change. When you are prompted to confirm that you are sure, click Yes. When the Operations Master is transferred, click OK.

26. Click Close to close the Change Schema Master dialog box.

27. Close the MMC console. If you are prompted to save the console settings, click No. Close the command prompt window.

End of exercise. Leave the windows open for the next exercise.

Exercise 16.4	Seizing Operations Masters
Overview	In this exercise, instead of transfering the Operations Master, you seize the Operations Masters and move them to another domain controller.
Mindset	It is always preferable to transfer roles instead of seizing roles. Transfer roles would be done when the current operations masters are available. Seizing a role is done when the operations masters are unavailable for a lengthy period of time and the operations masters are not available.
Completion time	10 minutes

1. On RWDC01, ensure that the Command Prompt (Admin) is open.

2. From the command prompt, execute the `ntdsutil` command.

3. At the ntdsutil prompt, execute the `roles` command.

4. At the fsmo maintenance prompt, execute the `connections` command.

5. At the server connections prompt, execute the following command:

   ```
   connect to server rwdc01
   ```

6. At the server connections prompt, execute the `quit` command.

7. To see the available options for fsmo maintenance, press the ? key and then press Enter.

8. To seize the roles, at the fsmo maintenance prompt, type the following commands:

   ```
   seize schema master

   seize naming master

   seize RID master

   seize PDC

   seize infrastructure master
   ```

   When an "Are you sure?" dialog box appears, click Yes to continue.

> **NOTE**
>
> *When you use the Ntdsutil.exe to seize an operations master role, Ntdsutil.exe will first try to transfer from the current role owner. If the current role owner is not available, the tool seizes the role. Remember, in production, you should only seize a role when the current holder will not be coming back any time soon.*

9. At the fsmo maintenance prompt, execute the `quit` command.

10. At the ntdsutil prompt, execute the `quit` command.

11. Close the command prompt.

End of exercise. Leave the windows open for the next exercise.

Exercise 16.5	Creating an RODC
Overview	In this exercise, you create and deploy a read-only domain controller (RODC).
Mindset	A Read-Only Domain Controller (RODC) contains a full replication of the domain database. However, it is placed where the physical security of the domain controller is not guaranteed. With an RODC available, Active Directory queries can be quicker than going to other sites over a slow WAN link.
Completion time	20 minutes

1. Log in to Server02 as the Contoso\administrator user account with the Pa$$w0rd password. The Server Manager console opens.

2. On Server Manager, click Manage > Add Roles and Features.

3. When the Add Roles and Features Wizard opens, click Next.

4. On the Select installation type page, click Next.

5. On the Select destination server page, click Next.

6. Click Active Directory Domain Services. When you are prompted to add features, click Add Features and then click Next.

7. On the Select features page, click Next.

8. On the Active Directory Domain Services page, click Next.

9. On the Confirm installation selections page, click Install.

10. When the installation is complete, click Close.

11. On the left pane, click AD DS. On the right-pane, in the yellow bar, click More.

12. In the All Servers Task Details window, click Promote this server to a domain controller. The Active Directory Domain Services Configuration Wizard starts.

13. On the Deployment Configuration page, confirm that Add a domain controller to an existing domain is already selected and then click Next.

14. On the Domain Controllers Options page, select Read only domain controller (RODC) and select the correct site name (Default-First-Site-Name, in this case). In the Password and Confirm Password text boxes, type **Pa$$w0rd,** as shown in Figure 16-3.

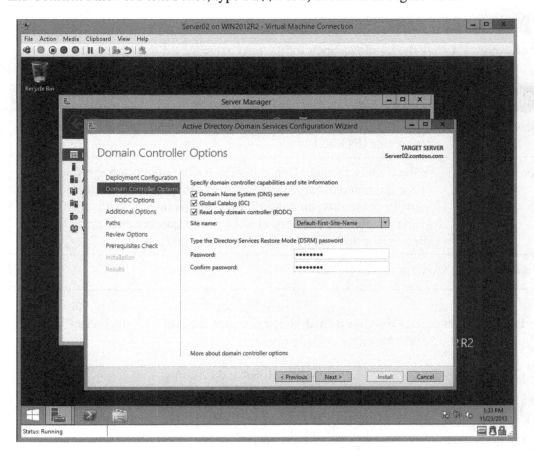

Figure 16-3
Promoting a server to a read-only domain controller

Question 3	*Which accounts can replicate passwords to the RODC?*

Question 4	*Which accounts are denied from replicating passwords?*

15. Click Next.

16. On the RODC Options page, under Delegated administrator account, click Select. In the text box, type **App1Service** and then click OK. Click Next.

17. On the Additional Options page, click Next.

18. On the Paths page, click Next.

19. On the Review Options page, click Next.

20. On the Prerequisites Check page, click Install.

21. When the installation is complete, Windows automatically restarts the domain controller.

22. On RWDC01, using Server Manager, click Tools > Active Directory Users and Computers.

23. Navigate to the Domain Controllers OU. Wait for Server02 to reboot. Then right-click Server02 and choose Properties. The Properties dialog box opens.

24. Click the Password Replication Policy tab to view the current password replication policies.

25. Take a screen shot of the Password Replication Policy tab by pressing Alt+Prt Scr and then paste it into your Lab16_worksheet file in the page provided by pressing Ctrl+V.

26. Click OK to close the Server02 Properties dialog box.

End of exercise.

LAB REVIEW QUESTIONS

Completion time	10 minutes

1. In Exercise 16.2, which tool was used to enable Universal Group Membership Caching?

2. In Exercise 16.3, how many PDC emulators are there within a typical organization?

3. In Exercise 16.3, when you try to transfer an operations master to another domain controller using an MMC and the source and target domain controllers are the same, what do you have to do?

4. In Exercise 16.3, to be able to access the Active Directory Schema console, what must you do first?

5. In Exercise 16.3, what did you use to transfer the PDC Emulator role?

6. In Exercise 16.4, what did you use to seize the operation masters?

7. In Exercise 16.5, where would you go if you need to modify which accounts are replicated to the RODC?

Lab Challenge	Cloning a Domain Controller
Overview	To complete this challenge, you must demonstrate how to clone a domain controller by writing the steps to complete the tasks described in the scenerio. Due to time, this is a written-only exercise.
Mindset	Starting with Windows Server 2012, you can safely virtualize a domain controller and rapidly deploy virtual domain controllers through cloning. It allows you to quickly restore domain controllers when a failure occurs and to rapidly provision a test environment when you need to deploy and test new features or capabilities before you apply the features or capabilities to production.
Completion time	20 minutes

Write out the steps you performed to complete the challenge.

End of lab.

LAB 17
MAINTAINING ACTIVE DIRECTORY

THIS LAB CONTAINS THE FOLLOWING EXERCISES AND ACTIVITIES:

Exercise 17.1   Backing Up System State

Exercise 17.2   Restoring the System State

Exercise 17.3   Using an Active Directory Snapshot

Exercise 17.4   Restoring a Deleted Object Using the Active Directory Recycle Bin

Exercise 17.5   Managing the Active Directory Database

Lab Challenge   Removing Server02 from Active Directory

BEFORE YOU BEGIN

The lab environment consists of student workstations connected to a local area network, along with a server that functions as the domain controller for a domain called *contoso.com*. The computers required for this lab are listed in Table 17-1.

Table 17-1
Computers Required for Lab 17

Computer	Operating System	Computer Name
Server (VM 1)	Windows Server 2012 R2	RWDC01
Server (VM 2)	Windows Server 2012 R2	Server01
Server (VM 3)	Windows Server 2012 R2	Server02

In addition to the computers, you also require the software listed in Table 17-2 to complete Lab 17.

Table 17-2
Software Required for Lab 17

Software	Location
Lab 17 student worksheet	Lab17_worksheet.docx (provided by instructor)

Working with Lab Worksheets

Each lab in this manual requires that you answer questions, take screen shots, and perform other activities that you will document in a worksheet named for the lab, such as Lab17_worksheet.docx. You will find these worksheets on the book companion site. It is recommended that you use a USB flash drive to store your worksheets, so you can submit them to your instructor for review. As you perform the exercises in each lab, open the appropriate worksheet file using Word, fill in the required information, and save the file to your flash drive.

After completing this lab, you will be able to:

- Back up the System State including Active Directory

- Perform an Active Directory restore

- Configure Active Directory snapshots

- Restore a Deleted Object using the Active Directory Recycle Bin

- Perform Active Directory maintenance

Estimated lab time: 130 minutes

Exercise 17.1	Backing Up System State
Overview	In this exercise, you will use Windows Server Backup to back up the system state of Server01, which includes the Active Directory.
Mindset	The system state is a collection of system components that make major components of Windows that cannot be easily backed up. It includes boot files, the registry, SYSVOL, Active Directory database, certificate store, and IIS metabase.
Completion time	30 minutes

Installing Windows Server Backup

Question 1	*What is the best method for disaster recovery?*

1. Log in to Server01 as the contoso\administrator user account and the Pa$$w0rd password. The Server Manager console opens.

2. On Server Manager, click Manage > Add Roles and Features.

3. When the Add Roles and Features Wizard starts, click Next.

4. On the Select installation type page, click Next.

5. On the Select destination server page, click Next.

6. On the Select server roles page, click Next.

7. On the Select features page, click to select the Windows Server Backup and then click Next.

8. On the Confirm installation selections page, click Install.

9. When the installation is complete, click Close.

Performing a Back Up of the System State

1. Log in to RWDC01 as the contoso\administrator user account and the Pa$$w0rd password. The Server Manager console opens.

2. On RWDC01, open Windows Explorer and create a **C:\BAK** folder.

3. Right-click the BAK folder and choose Properties.

4. When the Properties dialog box opens, click the Sharing tab.

5. Click Advanced Sharing.

6. When the Advanced Sharing dialog box opens, click Share this folder. Click Permissions and then click to select the Allow Full Control permission for Everyone. Click OK to close the Permissions for BAK dialog box and then click OK to close the Advanced Sharing dialog box.

7. Click Close to close the BAK Properties dialog box.

8. On Server01, using Server Manager, click Tools > Windows Server Backup. The Windows Server Backup console opens.

9. Click Local Backup in the left pane. Wait a moment while the data is being read.

10. Under Actions, click Backup Once.

11. When the Backup Once Wizard starts, ensure Different Options is selected and then click Next.

12. On the Select Backup Configuration page, click Custom and then click Next.

13. On the Select Items for Backup page, click Add Items. The Select Items dialog box opens as shown in Figure 17-1.

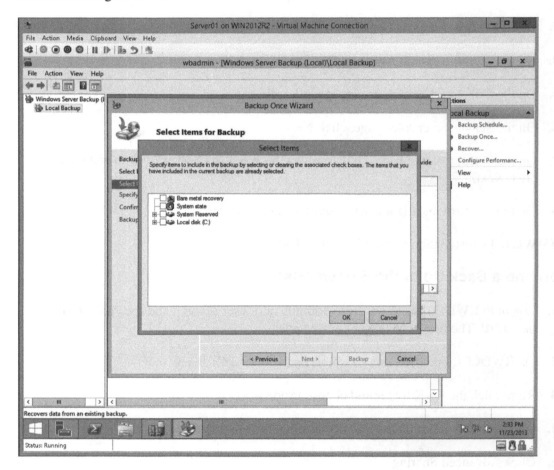

Figure 17-1
Selecting items for backup

14. Select System state and then click OK.

15. On the Select Items for Backup page, click Next.

16. On the Specify Destination Type page, select the Remote shared folder and then click Next.

17. On the Specify Remote Folder page, type **\\RWDC01\BAK** and then click Next.

18. On the Confirmation page, click Backup. The backup will take a few minutes.

19. When the backup is completed, take a screen shot of the Backup Once Wizard window by pressing Alt+Prt Scr and then paste it into your Lab17_worksheet file in the page provided by pressing Ctrl+V.

20. Click Close.

End of exercise. Leave the windows open for the next exercise.

Exercise 17.2	Restoring the System State
Overview	In the previous exercise, you performed a backup. In this exercise, you will perform a restore of the system state. However, before you perform the final reboot, you will make an OU authoritative so that the OU will not be overwritten by other domain controllers.
Mindset	When restoring Active Directory, there are nonauthoritative restores and authoritative restores. If a nonauthoritative restore is performed, Active Directory will overwrite the old data that is restored from backup. An authoritative restore is necessary when you want to restore old data as data that you want to keep.
Completion time	30 minutes

1. On Server01, using Server Manager, click Tools > Active Directory Users and Computers.

2. When the Active Directory Users and Computers console opens, navigate to the Service Accounts OU and delete the App1 Service account. Click Yes to confirm.

3. Close Active Directory Users and Computers.

4. On a physical server, you would normally press F8 during reboot. However, because you are running on a virtual environment on Server01, you need to right-click Start, choose Run, type **msconfig.exe,** and then click OK (to open System Configuration). Click the Boot tab, click to select Safe boot, and then select Active Directory repair. Click OK and then click Restart to restart the computer.

5. Log in as the local administrator (DSRM) using the Pa$$w0rd password.

6. On Server01, using Server Manager, click Tools > Windows Server Backup. The Windows Server Backup console opens.

7. Click Local Backup. After the data is read, under Actions, click Recover.

8. When the Recovery Wizard starts, select A backup stored on another location and click Next.

9. On the Specify Location Type page, click Remote shared folder and then click Next.

10. On the Specify Remote Folder page, type **\\RWDC01\BAK** and then click Next.

11. On the Select Backup Date page, select today's date of the backup that you want to restore from and then click Next.

12. On the Select Recovery Type page, click System state and then click Next.

13. On the Select Location for System State Recovery page, if you select Perform an authoritative restore of Active Directory files, the data contained on the domain controller for Active Directory would be considered authoritative after the restore and would overwrite Active Directory information on other domain controllers. Because you need only to restore the accounts in the Service Accounts OU, you do not have to select authoritative restore. Click Next.

14. When a warning displays, alerting you to the fact that this recovery option will cause all replicated content on the local server to re-synchronize after recovery, click OK.

15. When it you are prompted to confirm that you want to continue, click OK.

16. On the Confirmation page, click Recover.

17. When you are again prompted to confirm that you want to continue, click Yes.

18. If you receive a Server Manager System Error, do nothing; let the restore finish. When the restore is complete, reboot Server01. Remember that you will still reboot. If the System Manager System Error is not displayed, click Restart. If you cannot restart the computer because of lack of Windows controls, go to RWDC01, open Command Prompt (Admin), and then execute the following command:

```
shutdown /m \\server01 /r /f
```

19. After reboot, log in to Server01 as the local administrator (DSRM) with the password of Pa$$word.

20. Take a screen shot of the Command Prompt window by pressing Alt+Prt Scr and then paste it into your Lab17_worksheet file in the page provided by pressing Ctrl+V.

21. On the command prompt window, press Enter.

22. Right-click the Start menu and choose Command Prompt (Admin). The command prompt window opens.

23. Execute the **ntdsutil** command.

24. From the ntdsutil prompt, execute the **activate instance NTDS** command.

25. At the ntdsutil prompt, execute the **authoritative restore** command.

26. To mark the Service Accounts OU to be restored with an authoritative restore, execute the following command:

    ```
    restore subtree "OU=Service Accounts,DC=contoso,DC=com"
    ```

27. When the Authoritative Restore Confirmation dialog box opens, click Yes to perform the authoritative restore. When the record or records have been updated, the names of the back-link files are displayed.

28. Take a screen shot of the ntdsutil Command Prompt window by pressing Alt+Prt Scr and then paste it into your Lab17_worksheet file in the page provided by pressing Ctrl+V.

29. Execute the **quit** command twice to get back to the command prompt.

30. Execute **msconfig.exe**. Click the Boot tab, deselect the Safe boot option, and then click OK. When you are prompted to restart, click Restart.

31. Log in to Server01 as contoso\administrator with the password of Pa$$w0rd.

32. Using Server Manager, open Active Directory Users and Computers and verify that the App1 Service account is restored to the Service Accounts OU.

End of exercise. On Server01, close Active Directory Users and Computers.

Exercise 17.3	Using an Active Directory Snapshot
Overview	In this exercise, you will create a snapshot of Active Directory. You then mount and access the snapshot.
Mindset	Active Directory snapshots allow you to view Active Directory using tools such as Active Directory Users and Computers so that you can compare objects from the snapshot to your current Active Directory. The biggest limitation when using snapshots is that you cannot copy objects from the snapshot.
Completion time	20 minutes

1. On Server01, right-click the Start button and choose Command Prompt (Admin). The command prompt window opens.

2. At the command prompt, execute the **ntdsutil** command.

3. At the ntdsutil prompt, execute the **snapshot** command.

4. At the snapshot prompt, execute the **activate instance ntds** command.

5. Execute the **create** command.

Question 2	*What is the GUID (without the braces (}})) of the snapshot created?*

6. To return a list of all snapshots, at the snapshot prompt, execute the **list all** command.

7. Execute the **mount {GUID}** command, where GUID is the one that you recorded. Do not type the braces ({ })

8. Take a screen shot of the ntdsutil Command Prompt window by pressing Alt+Prt Scr and then paste it into your Lab17_worksheet file in the page provided by pressing Ctrl+V.

9. Execute the **quit** command twice to exit ntdsutil.

10. To mount the snapshot, execute the following command:

```
dsamain -dbpath
c:\$snap_datetime_volumec$\windows\ntds\ntds.dit
-ldapport 5000
```

You need to specify the date-time when you performed the mount command. The port number (5000) can be any open and unique TCP port number (see Figure 17-2).

Figure 17-2
Mounting a snapshot

11. A message indicates that Active Directory Domain Services startup is complete. Do not close the command prompt window; leave the command you just ran, dsamain.exe, running while you continue to the next step.

12. Using Server Manager, click Tools > Active Directory Users and Computers. The Active Directory Users and Computers console opens.

13. Right-click contoso.com and choose Change Domain Controller. The Change Directory Server dialog box appears.

14. Click <Type a Directory Server name[:port] here>, type **Server01.contoso.com:5000**, and then press Enter.

15. Click OK when it becomes available. You are now viewing the snapshot. Therefore, you can navigate to any organizational unit and view the users and computers.

16. Go to the command prompt in which the snapshot is mounted.

17. Press Ctrl+C to stop DSAMain.exe.

18. Execute the **ntdsutil** command.

19. Execute the **activate instance ntds** command.

20. Execute the **snapshot** command.

21. Type **unmount <GUID>**, where GUID is the GUID of the snapshot, and then press Enter.

22. Execute the **list all** command.

23. Because the snapshot is the first entry in the list, execute the **delete 1** command:

24. Execute the **quit** command twice.

25. Take a screen shot of the ntdsutil Command Prompt window by pressing Alt+Prt Scr and then paste it into your Lab17_worksheet file in the page provided by pressing Ctrl+V.

End of exercise. Close the command prompt window and close the Active Directory Users and Computers console.

Exercise 17.4	Restoring a Deleted Object Using the Active Directory Recycle Bin
Overview	In this exercise, you will activate the Active Directory Recycle Bin. You will then delete an object and restore the object from the Recycle Bin.
Mindset	Similar to the Windows Recycle Bin, deleted objects are stored in a deleted folder. For a period of time, after an Active Directory object has been deleted, an administrator can undelete an object, restoring it to the state at which it was when it was deleted.
Completion time	10 minutes

1. On Server01, using Server Manager, click Tools > Active Directory Administrative Center. The Active Directory Administrative Center opens.

2. Click contoso (local), as shown in Figure 17-3.

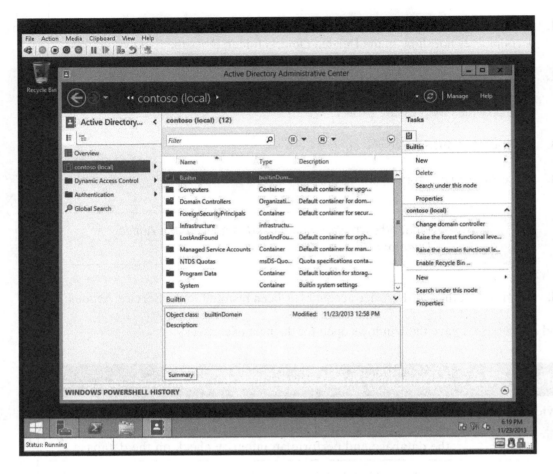

Figure 17-3
Managing the contoso domain with Active Directory Administrator Center

3. In the right pane, click Enable Recycle Bin. When you are presented with a message that states that once the Recycle Bin has been enabled, it cannot be disabled and prompts you to confirm that you want to continue, click OK.

4. When you are prompted to confirm that you want to refresh the AD Administrative Center now, click OK.

5. Press the F5 key on the keyboard to refresh the Active Directory Administrative Center.

6. Using Server Manager, open Active Directory Users and Computers.

7. Expand contoso.com and then click Service Accounts.

8. Delete the App1Service account. Click Yes to continue.

9. Close Active Directory Users and Computers.

10. Go back to the Active Directory Administrative Center.

11. Click the small arrow next to the domain and select Deleted Objects. If the App1Service account does not show in the Deleted Objects folder, press the F5 key to refresh.

12. Take a screen shot of Deleted Objects in the Active Directory Administrative Center window by pressing Alt+Prt Scr and then paste it into your Lab17_worksheet file in the page provided by pressing Ctrl+V.

13. Right-click App1Service and choose Restore.

14. Close Active Directory Administrative Center.

Question 3	*What other method could used to activate the Active Directory Recycle Bin?*

15. Confirm that the App1Service account has been restored to the Service Accounts OU.

End of exercise. Leave the windows open for the next exercise.

Exercise 17.5	Managing the Active Directory Database
Overview	From time to time, you should perform maintenance on the Active Directory Database. Therefore, in this exercise, you will compact the database and perform an integrity check on the database.
Mindset	The Active Directory Database contains objects that are constantly changing; objects are created and deleted often. Therefore, to keep a database running efficiently, you should compress the database from time to time and make sure that there are no errors within the database.
Completion time	20 minutes

1. On Server01, using Server Manager, click Tools > Services. The Services console opens.

2. Right-click the Active Directory Domain Services service and choose Stop. When you are prompted to confirm that you want to stop other services, click Yes.

3. Right-click the Start button and choose Command Prompt (Admin). The command prompt window opens.

4. Execute the **ntdsutil** command.

5. At the ntdsutil prompt, execute the **activate instance NTDS** command.

6. Execute the **files** command.

7. At the file maintenance prompt, execute the **compact to C:** command. The database is compacted.

8. Take a screen shot of the ntdsutil Command Prompt window by pressing Alt+Prt Scr and then paste it into your Lab17_worksheet file in the page provided by pressing Ctrl+V.

9. To check the integrity of the offline database, execute the **integrity** command.

10. At the file maintenance prompt, execute the **quit** command.

11. To perform a semantic database consistency check, execute the **semantic database analysis** command.

12. At the semantic checker prompt, execute the **go** command.

13. Execute the **quit** command twice.

14. Copy the ntdis.dit file from the C:\ folder to the C:\Windows\NTDS folder.

15. Close the command prompt.

16. Go back to the Services console. Right-click the Active Directory Domain Services service and choose Start.

17. Close the Services console.

End of exercise.

LAB REVIEW QUESTIONS

Completion time	10 minutes

1. In Exercise 17.1, what did you use to back up the System State?

2. In Exercise 17.2, what type of restore will have changes overwritten by the current Active Directory?

3. In Exercise 17.2, when you restore from backup and you want to make sure that the restored objects in Active Directory do not get removed automatically by Active Directory because they were deleted in the past, what type of of restore must be done?

4. In Exercise 17.2, what tool allowed you to choose selected objects as authoritative restore?

5. In Exercise 17.3, what command did you use to create the Active Directory snapshot?

6. In Exercise 17.4, what did you use to enable the Active Directory Recycle Bin?

7. In Exercise 17.5, what program allowed you to compress the Active Directory database?

Lab Challenge	Removing Server02 from Active Directory
Overview	To complete this challenge, you will remove a domain controller from Active Directory.
Mindset	In Hyper V, you decide to shut down Server02 because it has been giving you problems that you cannot recover from. Assuming the Server02 is not available, how would you remove Server02 from Active Directory?
Completion time	10 minutes

Write out the steps you performed to complete the challenge.

End of lab.

LAB 18
CONFIGURING
ACCOUNT POLICIES

THIS LAB CONTAINS THE FOLLOWING EXERCISES AND ACTIVITIES:

Exercise 18.1   Configuring a Domain Password Policy

Exercise 18.2   Configuring Account Lockout Settings

Exercise 18.3   Configuring a Password Settings Object

Exercise 18.4   Configuring Kerberos Policy Settings

Lab Challenge   Managing Password Settings Objects Permissions

BEFORE YOU BEGIN

The lab environment consists of student workstations connected to a local area network, along with a server that functions as the domain controller for a domain called *contoso.com*. The computers required for this lab are listed in Table 18-1.

Table 18-1
Computers Required for Lab 18

Computer	Operating System	Computer Name
Server (VM 1)	Windows Server 2012 R2	RWDC01

In addition to the computers, you also require the software listed in Table 18-2 to complete Lab 18.

Table 18-2
Software Required for Lab 18

Software	Location
Lab 18 student worksheet	Lab18_worksheet.docx (provided by instructor)

Working with Lab Worksheets

Each lab in this manual requires that you answer questions, take screen shots, and perform other activities that you will document in a worksheet named for the lab, such as Lab18_worksheet.docx. You will find these worksheets on the book companion site. It is recommended that you use a USB flash drive to store your worksheets, so you can submit them to your instructor for review. As you perform the exercises in each lab, open the appropriate worksheet file using Word, fill in the required information, and save the file to your flash drive.

After completing this lab, you will be able to:

- Configure a domain user password policy

- Configure account lockout settings

- Configure and apply Password Settings Objects (PSOs)

- Configure Kerberos Policy Settings

Estimated lab time: 65 minutes

Exercise 18.1	Configuring a Domain Password Policy
Overview	In this exercise, you will define a domain-level password policy including maximum password length and password history.
Mindset	You can define only account policies, which include password policy, account lockout policy, and Kerberos policy, at the domain level. Because most organizations will have only one domain, you can set only one.
Completion time	10 minutes

1. Log in to RWDC01 as the Contoso\Administrator user account with the Pa$$w0rd password. The Server Manager console opens.

2. On Server Manager, click Tools > Group Policy Management. The Group Policy Management console opens.

3. Navigate to and right-click Default Domain Policy and choose Edit. The Group Policy Management Editor opens.

4. In the left window pane, expand the Computer Configuration node, expand the Policies node, and expand the Windows Settings folder. Then expand the Security Settings node. In the Security Settings node, expand Account Policies and select Password Policy, as shown in Figure 18-1.

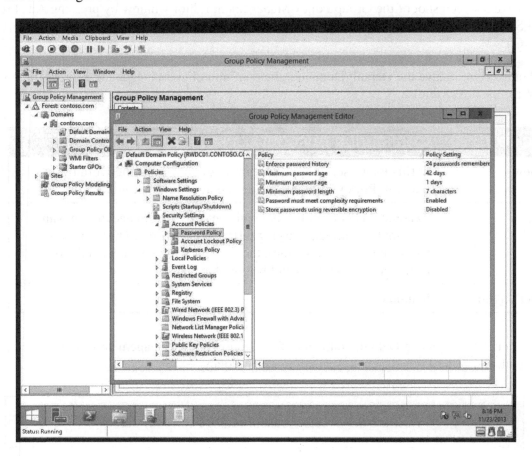

Figure 18-1
Managing Password Policy

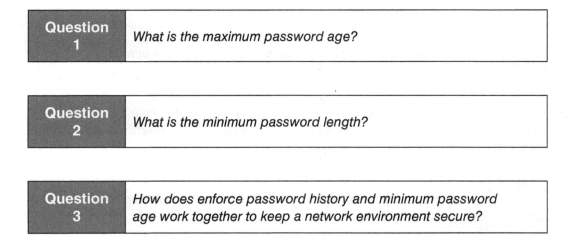

Question 1	*What is the maximum password age?*

Question 2	*What is the minimum password length?*

Question 3	*How does enforce password history and minimum password age work together to keep a network environment secure?*

5. Double-click the Minimum password length. When the Minimum password length Properties dialog box opens, change the 7 value to 8 characters. Click OK to close the Minimum password length Properties dialog box.

6. Take a screen shot of the Group Policy Management Editor window by pressing Alt+Prt Scr and then paste it into your Lab18_worksheet file in the page provided by pressing Ctrl+V.

End of exercise. Leave the Default Domain Policy Group Policy Management Editor window open for the next exercise.

Exercise 18.2	Configuring Account Lockout Settings
Overview	In this exercise, you will continue to configure the Default Domain Policy by configuring the account lockout settings.
Mindset	Account lockout settings help prevent a user from hacking into an account by continually trying different passwords. Therefore, if a hacker fails too many times, the account will be locked, and any further attempts will be not be possible.
Completion time	5 minutes

1. On RWDC01, using Default Domain Policy Group Policy Management Editor console, under Account Policies, click Account Lockout Policy.

Question 4	How are the account lockout settings currently set?

2. Double-click Account lockout duration. When the Account lockout duration Properties dialog box opens, click to enable the Define this policy setting.

Question 5	What is the default value for the Account lockout duration?

3. Click OK to close the Account lockout duration Properties dialog box. When the Suggested Value Changes dialog box opens, look at the suggested settings and then click OK.

Question 6	How many invalid logon attempts can be made that will cause an account to be locked?

4. Take a screen shot of the Account Lockout Policy window by pressing Alt+Prt Scr and then paste it into your Lab18_worksheet file in the page provided by pressing Ctrl+V.

5. Close the Group Policy Management Editor window for the Default Domain Policy.

6. Close the Group Policy Management console.

End of exercise.

Exercise 18.3	Configuring a Password Settings Object
Overview	In this exercise, you will create and apply a Password Settings Object to the Sales group.
Mindset	Password Settings Objects (PSOs) are created and assigned to user objects or global security groups. These settings will overwrite the domain level settings for security settings, including the password policies and account lockout settings.
Completion time	25 minutes

1. On RWDC01, using Server Manager, click Tools > Active Directory Users and Computers. The Active Directory Users and Computers console opens.

2. Right-click contoso.com and choose New > Organizational Unit.

3. When the New Object – Organizational Unit dialog box opens, type **Sales** in the Name text box. Click OK to close the New Object – Organizational Unit dialog box.

4. Right-click the Sales organizational unit and choose New > User. The New Object – User dialog box opens.

5. Type the following information:

   First name: **John**

   Last name: **Smith**

   User logon name: **JSmith**

   Click Next.

6. For the Password and Confirm password text boxes, type **Pa$$w0rd**.

7. Click to select the Password never expires. When the warning appears, click OK. Click Next.

8. Click Finish.

9. Create a user in the Sales OU with the following information:

   First name: **Stacy**

   Last name: **Jones**

   User logon name: **SJones**

   Password: **Pa$$w0rd**

   Select Password never expires and then click Finish to close the New Object – User dialog box.

10. Right-click the Sales OU and choose New > Group. The New Object – Group dialog box opens.

11. In the Group name text box, type **Sales** and then click OK.

12. Double-click the Sales group. The Sales Properties dialog opens.

13. Click the Members tab.

14. Click Add. The Select Users, Contacts, Computers, Service Accounts, or Groups dialog box opens.

15. In the text box, type **John Smith; Stacy Jones** and then click OK.

16. Take a screen shot of the Sales Properties dialog box window by pressing Alt+Prt Scr and then paste it into your Lab18_worksheet file in the page provided by pressing Ctrl+V.

17. Click OK to close the Sales Properties dialog box.

18. On RWDC01, using Server Manager, click Tools > Active Directory Administrative Center. The Active Directory Administrative Center opens.

19. In the Active Directory Administrative Center navigation pane, click the arrow next to the contoso.com (local) and select the System folder. Then scroll down and double-click Password Settings Container. The Password Settings Container is shown in Figure 18-2.

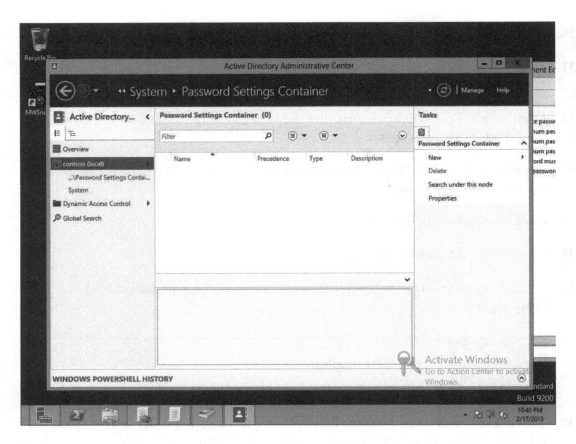

Figure 18-2
Managing Password Settings Container

20. In the Tasks pane, click New > Password Settings. The Create Password Settings window opens.

21. In the Name text box, type **PSO1**.

22. In the Precedence text box, type **1**.

23. Change the minimum password length to **12**.

24. Click to enable Enforce account lockout policy.

25. Set the Number of failed logon attempts to **3**.

26. Change both the Reset failed logon attempts count after and Account will be locked out for a duration of **15** minutes.

27. In the Directly Applies To section, click the Add button.

28. When the Select Users or Groups dialog box opens, type **Sales** in the text box and then click OK.

29. Click OK to submit the creation of the PSO.

30. Close the Active Directory Administrative Center.

31. Using Server Manager, open Tools > Active Directory Users and Computers. The Active Directory Users and Computers console opens.

32. Open the View menu and make sure that Advanced Features is checked. If it is not, click the Advanced Features option.

33. Open the Sales OU and then right-click John Smith and choose Properties. The user Properties dialog box opens.

34. Click the Attribute Editor tab.

35. Click Filter, and click Constructed.

36. Scroll down and find the msDS-ResultantPSO attribute to see the current PSO being applied.

Question 7	Which PSO is applied?

37. Take a screen shot of the Attribute Editor tab by pressing Alt+Prt Scr and then paste it into your Lab18_worksheet file in the page provided by pressing Ctrl+V.

38. Clicked OK to close the Properties dialog box.

39. Close the Active Directory Users and Computers console.

End of exercise.

Exercise 18.4	Configuring Kerberos Policy Settings
Overview	In this exercise, configure Kerberos Policy settings using the default domain policy.
Mindset	Kerberos is the default authentication mechanism in an Active Directory Domain services (AD DS) environment and plays a critical role in authorization and auditing. Because Kerberos is used as part of the Active Directory domain, Kerberos settings can be configured only at the domain level with a GPO.
Completion time	10 minutes

1. On RWDC01, using Group Policy Management, navigate to and right-click Default Domain Policy and choose Edit. The Group Policy Management Editor opens.

2. In the left window pane, expand the Computer Configuration node, expand the Policies node, and expand the Windows Settings folder. Then expand the Security Settings node. In the Security Settings node, expand Account Policies and select Kerberos Policy.

Question 8	*What is the maximum tolerance for computer clock synchronization?*

3. Double-click Maximum tolerance for computer clock synchronization.

4. When the Maximum tolerance for computer clock synchronization dialog box opens, change the maximum tolerance to 4 minutes. Click OK.

5. Double-click Maximum lifetime for user ticket.

6. When the Maximum lifetime for user ticket Properties dialog box opens, change the time to 8 hours. Click OK.

7. When the Suggested Value Changes dialog box opens, click OK.

8. Take a screen shot of the Group Policy Management Editor by pressing Alt+Prt Scr and then paste it into your Lab18_worksheet file in the page provided by pressing Ctrl+V.

9. Close Group Policy Management Editor.

End of exercise.

LAB REVIEW QUESTIONS

Completion time	5 minutes

1. In Exercise 18.1, what did you use to define Password policies?

2. In Exercise 18.1, for a domain, where do you define password policies?

3. In Exercise 18.3, what are Password Settings Objects assigned to?

4. In Exercise 18.3, which settings are configured with Password Settings Objects?

Lab Challenge	Managing Password Settings Objects Permissions
Overview	To complete this challenge, you must demonstrate how to manage Password Settings Object Permissions by writing the steps to complete the tasks described in the scenerio.
Mindset	As an administrator for the Contoso Corporation, how would you delegate permissions so that John Smith could manage the Password Settings Objects for the Contoso.com domain?
Completion time	10 minutes

Write out the steps you performed to complete the challenge.

End of lab.

LAB 19
CONFIGURING GROUP POLICY PROCESSING

THIS LAB CONTAINS THE FOLLOWING EXERCISES AND ACTIVITIES: _ _ _ _

Exercise 19.1   Configuring Processing and Precedence of GPOs

Exercise 19.2   Configuring Blocking Inheritance and Enforced Policies

Exercise 19.3   Configuring Security Filtering and WMI Filtering

Exercise 19.4   Configuring Loopback Processing

Lab Challenge   Using Group Policy Results Wizard

BEFORE YOU BEGIN

The lab environment consists of student workstations connected to a local area network, along with a server that functions as the domain controller for a domain called *contoso.com*. The computers required for this lab are listed in Table 19-1.

Table 19-1
Computers Required for Lab 19

Computer	Operating System	Computer Name
Server (VM 1)	Windows Server 2012 R2	RWDC01

In addition to the computers, you also require the software listed in Table 19-2 to complete Lab 19.

Table 19-2
Software Required for Lab 19

Software	Location
Lab 19 student worksheet	Lab19_worksheet.docx (provided by instructor)

Working with Lab Worksheets

Each lab in this manual requires that you answer questions, shoot screen shots, and perform other activities that you will document in a worksheet named for the lab, such as Lab19_worksheet.docx. You will find these worksheets on the book companion site. It is recommended that you use a USB flash drive to store your worksheets, so you can submit them to your instructor for review. As you perform the exercises in each lab, open the appropriate worksheet file using Word, fill in the required information, and save the file to your flash drive.

After completing this lab, you will be able to:

- Configure the processing order and precedence of GPOs

- Configure blocking of inheritance and enforced policies

- Configure security and WMI filtering

- Configure loopback processing

Estimated lab time: 60 minutes

Exercise 19.1	Configuring Processing and Precedence of GPOs
Overview	During this exercise, you create multiple GPOs and look at overall precedence of the GPOs.
Mindset	Group policies are applied from top to bottom. In general, when a GPO is executed after an earlier executed GPO, the GPO executed later overwrites conflicting settings. If there is more than one GPO at a level, each GPO will be processed as specified by the precedence level.
Completion time	20 minutes

1. Log in to RWDC01 as the Contoso\administrator user account with the Pa$$word password. The Server Manager console opens.

2. Using Server Manager, click Tools > Active Directory Users and Computers. The Active Directory Users and Computers console opens.

3. If the Sales OU does not exist, create the Sales OU.

4. Under the Sales OU, create an East OU and a West OU.

5. Using Server Manager, click Tools > Group Policy Management. The Group Policy Management console opens.

6. Navigate to and click the Sales OU.

7. Right-click the Sales OU and choose Create a GPO in this domain, and Link it here. When the New GPO dialog box opens, type **GPO1** and then click OK.

8. Create a GPO named **GPO2** for West OU.

9. Create a GPO named **GPO3** for the East OU.

10. Create a GPO named **GPO4** for the contoso.com domain.

11. Create a GPO named **GPO5** for the Sales OU.

12. Create a GPO named **GPO6** for the East OU.

13. Create a GPO named **GPO7** for the East OU.

14. Click East OU, as shown in Figure 19-1. In the East pane, click Group Policy Inheritance.

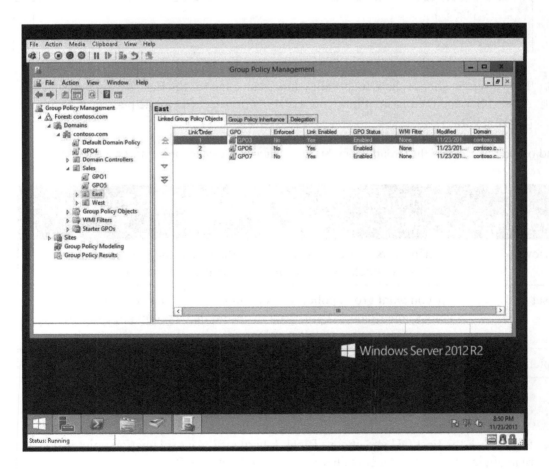

Figure 19-1
Viewing GPOs linked to a OU

Question 1	What is the order of GPOs that are being applied?

15. For the East OU, click Linked Group Policy Objects.

Question 2	What are the three GPOs linked to the East OU? List them in order?

16. Click GPO7 and then click the double up arrow.

Question 3	What are the three GPOs linked to the East OU? List them in order?

17. Click the Group Policy Inheritance tab.

Question 4	What is the order of GPOs that are being applied?

18. Take a screen shot of the Group Policy Inheritance tab for the East OU by pressing Alt+Prt Scr and then paste it into your Lab19_worksheet file in the page provided by pressing Ctrl+V.

End of exercise. Leave the Group Policy Management console open for the next exercise.

Exercise 19.2	Configuring Blocking Inheritance and Enforced Policies
Overview	During this exercise, you modify the order and precedence of GPOs by blocking inheritance and using enforced policies.
Mindset	If you want group policies to stop inheriting, you can actually use block inheritance. If you want to ensure that a group policy is not overwritten, you can select enforced.
Completion time	10 minutes

1. On RWDC01, with Group Policy Management, navigate to and click the East OU.

2. Right-click the East OU and choose Block Inheritance. An exclamation point inside a blue circle appears for the container as shown in Figure 19-2.

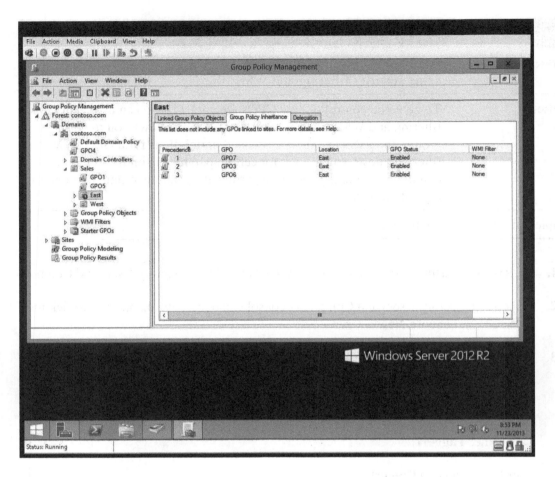

Figure 19-2
Viewing the East OU with block inheritance

3. Click the Group Policy Inheritance tab.

Question 5	What is the order of GPOs that are being applied to the East OU?

4. Right-click GPO4 and choose Enforced.

Question 6	What is the order of GPOs that are being applied to the East OU? *Note: You might need to press F5 key to refresh the screen.*

5. Take a screen shot of the Group Policy Inheritance tab for the East OU by pressing Alt+Prt Scr and then paste it into your Lab19_worksheet file in the page provided by pressing Ctrl+V.

End of exercise. Leave the Group Policy Management console open for the next exercise.

Exercise 19.3	Configuring Security Filtering and WMI Filtering
Overview	During this exercise, you fine-tune the processing of GPOs by using security filtering and WMI filtering.
Mindset	To give you control of how GPOs are applied, you can use security filtering and WMI filtering. Security filtering allows you to define groups and users and their associated permissions for a GPO. WMI filtering allows you to look for certain parameters on the computer that they are running such as a particular operating system or a certain type of hardware.
Completion time	10 minutes

1. On RWDC01, using Server Manager, click Tools > Active Directory Users and Computers.

2. In Active Directory Users and Computers console, under Contoso.com, right-click the Sales OU and choose New > User.

3. When the New Object – User dialog box opens, type the following information and click Next:

   First name: **Jason**

   Last name: **Taggert**

   User logon name: **JTaggert**

4. In the Password and Confirm password text boxes, type **Pa$$w0rd**.

5. Click the Password never expires option. When a warning appears, click OK and then click Next.

6. When the wizard is complete, click Finish.

7. Using Group Policy Management, click GPO5 that is assigned to the Sales OU. If needed, click OK on the message box that appears.

8. Click the Delegation tab and then click Advanced. The GPO Security Settings dialog box opens as shown in Figure 19-3.

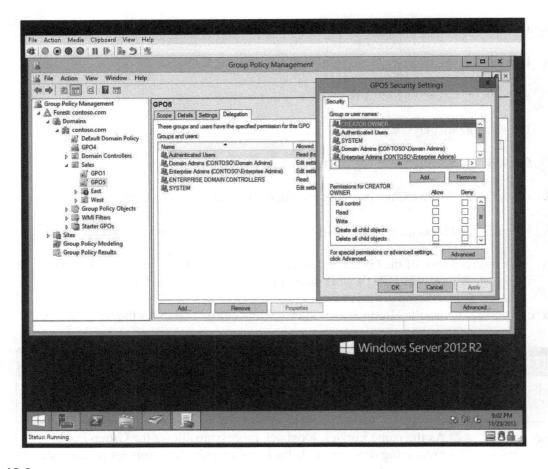

Figure 19-3
Viewing a GPO security settings

Question 7	*Which permissions are needed for a GPO to apply to a user?*

9. Click the Add button. The Select users, Computers, Service Accounts, or Groups dialog box opens.

10. In the text box, type **Jason Taggert** and then press Enter.

11. With Jason Taggert highlighted, assign the Deny Apply group policy and then click OK. When it states that Deny entries take precedence and prompts you to confirm if you want to continue, click Yes.

12. In the left pane, navigate to and click the WMI filters.

13. Right-click the WMI Filters node and choose New. The New WMI Filter dialog box opens.

14. In the Name and Description fields, type **WMIFilter1** in each text box.

15. In the Queries section, click Add. The WMI Query dialog box opens.

16. In the Query text box, type the following and then click OK:

    ```
    Select * from Win32_Processor where AddressWidth='32'
    ```

    If a warning displays, click OK.

17. Click Save to create the WMI filter.

18. Click GPO5. If a message box appears, click OK. Click the Scope tab.

19. Under WMI Filtering, select WMIFilter1. Click Yes to confirm your changes.

20. Take a screen shot of the GPO5 Scope tab for the Sales OU by pressing Alt+Prt Scr and then paste it into your Lab 19 worksheet file in the page provided by pressing Ctrl+V.

End of exercise. Leave the Group Policy Management console open for the next exercise.

Exercise 19.4	Configuring Loopback Processing
Overview	In this exercise, you will configure the computer settings to overwrite the user settings when applying GPO settings.
Mindset	As the name implies, loopback processing allows the Group Policy processing order to circle back and reapply the computer policies after all user policies and logon scripts run. It is intended to keep the configuration of the computer the same regardless of who logs on.
Completion time	5 minutes

1. On RWDC01, with Group Policy Management, click GPO1. If a message box appears, click OK.

2. Right-click GPO1 and choose Edit. The Group Policy Management Editor opens.

3. Navigate to and double-click Computer Configuration\Policies\Administrative Templates\System\Group Policy\Configure user Group Policy Loopback processing mode.

4. When the Configure user Group Policy loopback processing mode dialog opens, click Enabled.

Question 8	What is the difference between Replace and Merge?

5. Change the mode to Merge.

6. Take a screen shot of the Configure user Group Policy loopback processing mode dialog box window by pressing Alt+Prt Scr and then paste it into your Lab19_worksheet file in the page provided by pressing Ctrl+V.

7. Click OK and then close the Group Policy Management Editor and the Group Policy Management console.

End of exercise.

LAB REVIEW QUESTIONS

Completion time	5 minutes

1. In Exercise 19.1, which policy has the highest precedence?

2. In Exercise 19.2, how do you make sure that a GPO that is assigned at the domain level is not overwritten by GPOs at a lower level?

3. In Exercise 19.3, where do you define the security filtering of GPOs?

4. In Exercise 19.4, how do you ensure computer settings are applied after user settings?

Lab Challenge	Using Group Policy Results Wizard
Overview	To complete this challenge, you will demonstrate how to use the Group Policy Results Wizard to view current GPO settings being applied to a user.
Minset	Over the last few months, you and your team have created and applied over 30 GPOs. However, you are getting a little bit confused on which GPOs are being applied. What can you do to determine which GPOs are being applied?
Completion time	10 minutes

Write out the steps you performed to complete the challenge.

End of lab.

LAB 20
CONFIGURING GROUP POLICY SETTINGS

THIS LAB CONTAINS THE FOLLOWING EXERCISES AND ACTIVITIES:

Exercise 20.1   Performing Software Installation with Group Policies

Exercise 20.2   Using Folder Redirection

Exercise 20.3   Using Scripts with Group Policies

Exercise 20.4   Using Administrative Templates

Exercise 20.5   Using Security Templates

Lab Challenge   Using ADM Files

BEFORE YOU BEGIN

The lab environment consists of student workstations connected to a local area network, along with a server that functions as the domain controller for a domain called *contoso.com*. The computers required for this lab are listed in Table 20-1.

Table 20-1
Computers Required for Lab 20

Computer	Operating System	Computer Name
Server (VM 1)	Windows Server 2012 R2	RWDC01
Server (VM 2)	Windows Server 2012 R2	Server01

In addition to the computers, you also require the software listed in Table 20-2 to complete Lab 20.

Table 20-2
Software Required for Lab 20

Software	Location
System Center Monitoring Pack for File and Storage Management.msi	\\RWDC01\Software
ADMX Migrator	\\RWDC01\Software
Lab 20 student worksheet	Lab20_worksheet.docx (provided by instructor)

Working with Lab Worksheets

Each lab in this manual requires that you answer questions, take screen shots, and perform other activities that you will document in a worksheet named for the lab, such as Lab20_worksheet.docx. You will find these worksheets on the book companion site. It is recommended that you use a USB flash drive to store your worksheets, so you can submit them to your instructor for review. As you perform the exercises in each lab, open the appropriate worksheet file using Word, fill in the required information, and save the file to your flash drive.

After completing this lab, you will be able to:

- Perform software installation with group policies

- Use folder redirection

- Run scripts with group policies

- Configure administrative and security templates

Estimated lab time: 75 minutes

Exercise 20.1	Performing Software Installation with Group Policies
Overview	During this exercise, you will perform a software installation of an MSI file using group policies.
Mindset	When you install software with GPOs, you have the choice to install software to a computer or to a user. You also have the choice to assign the software or publish software.
Completion time	10 minutes

1. Log in to RWDC01 as the Contoso\Administrator user account with the Pa$$w0rd password. The Server Manager console opens.

2. Using Server Manager, under Tools, open Active Directory Users and Computers.

3. Right-click contoso.com and choose New > Organizational Unit. Then create an organizational unit called Eng.

4. Right-click the Eng OU and choose New > User.

5. When the New Object – User dialog box opens, type the following information and click Next:

    First name: **Ted**

    Last name: **Reynolds**

    User logon name: **TReynolds**

6. In the Password and Confirm password text boxes, type **Pa$$w0rd**.

7. Click the Password never expires check box. When a warning appears, click OK. Click Next.

8. When the wizard is complete, click Finish.

9. Using Active Directory Users and Computers, move Server02 to the Eng OU.

10. Close Active Directory Users and Computers.

11. Using Server Manager, click Tools > Group Policy Management.

12. Right-click the organizational unit called Eng and choose Create a GPO in this domain, and Link it here.

13. When the New GPO dialog box opens, for the Name, type **GPO20** and then click OK.

14. Right-click GPO20 and choose Edit. If a pop up window opens, click OK. The Group Policy Management Editor opens.

15. Navigate to Software Settings under the Computer Configuration\Policies\Software Settings.

16. Right-click the Software installation node and choose New > Package. The Open dialog box opens.

17. Navigate to the \\RWDC01\Software. Click System Center Monitoring Pack for File and Storage Management and then click Open.

Question 1	*What happens when software is assigned to a computer using a GPO?*

Question 2	*Why is Published grayed out?*

18. When the Deploy Software dialog box opens (as shown in Figure 20-1), ensure that Assigned is selected, and click OK. The System Center Monitoring Pack for File and Storage Management appears in the right pane of the Group Policy Management Editor. Ensure that the Software installation node is selected in the left pane.

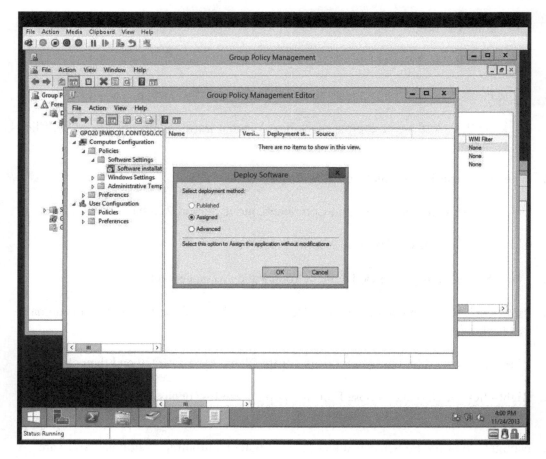

Figure 20-1
Selecting a deployment method

19. Take a screen shot of the Group Policy Management Editor showing the Software Installation pane by pressing Alt+Prt Scr and then paste it into your Lab20_worksheet file in the page provided by pressing Ctrl+V.

End of exercise. Leave the Group Policy Management Editor window open for the next exercise.

Exercise 20.2	Using Folder Redirection
Overview	In this exercise, you will create a UserData folder on a server and redirect the user's Documents folder to the UserData folder.
Mindset	By having a Documents folder located centrally, you can easily back up these documents. This is particularly useful for laptop users who might not always be in the office and don't have the opportunity to back up the files.
Completion time	10 minutes

1. Log in to Server01 as the Contoso\Administrator user account with the Pa$$w0rd password. The Server Manager console opens.

2. On Server01, create the C:\UserData folder.

3. Right-click the C:\UserData folder and choose Properties. The Properties dialog box opens.

4. Click the Sharing tab and then click Advanced Sharing. The Advanced Sharing dialog box opens.

5. Click Share this folder. Click Permissions and then click Allow Full Control permission for Everyone.

6. Take a screen shot of the Permissions for UserData dialog box by pressing Alt+Prt Scr and then paste it into your Lab20_worksheet file in the page provided by pressing Ctrl+V.

7. Click OK to close the Permissions for UserData dialog box and then click OK to close the Advanced Sharing dialog box.

8. Click Close to close the UserData Properties dialog box.

9. On RWDC01, using Group Policy Management Editor for GPO20, navigate to and expand the \User Configuration\Policies\Windows Settings\Folder Redirection node.

10. Right-click the Documents folder in the left window pane and choose Properties. The Documents Properties dialog box opens as shown in Figure 20-2.

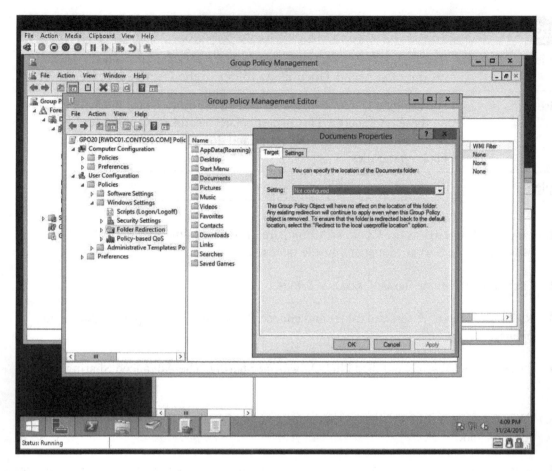

Figure 20-2
Redirecting the Documents folder

11. Under Setting, click the down-arrow and choose Basic – Redirect everyone's folder to the same location. Under Root Path, type **\\server01\UserData**.

Question 3	If a domain user (for example, JSmith) logs in, where would his Documents folder be located?

12. Click OK to close Documents Properties dialog box. If a warning appears, prompting you to confirm that you want to continue, click Yes.

13. Log in to Server02 as contoso\TReynolds with the password of Pa$$w0rd.

14. Open File Explorer.

15. Right-click the Documents folder under This PC in the left pane, and choose Properties.

16. Take a screen shot of the Documents Properties dialog box by pressing Alt+Prt Scr and then paste it into your Lab20_worksheet file in the page provided by pressing Ctrl+V.

17. Click OK to close the Documents Properties dialog box.

End of exercise. Leave all servers logged in and keep the Group Policy Management Editor window open for the next exercise.

Exercise 20.3	Using Scripts with Group Policies
Overview	In this exercise, you will create a simple login script that will map the G drive to a shared folder.
Mindset	You can assign startup and shutdown scripts to a computer and assign logon and logoff scripts to a user. Whenever a computer starts, the startup script will be executed. Whenever a computer is shutting down properly, the shutdown script is executed. Similarly, when a user logs on, the logon script is executed. When a user logs off, the logoff script is executed.
Completion time	10 minutes

1. On Server01, create the C:\Stuff folder

2. Right-click the Stuff folder and choose Properties.

3. Click the Sharing tab and then click Advanced Sharing. The Advanced Sharing dialog box opens. Then click Share this folder.

4. Click Permissions. Click Allow Full Control permission for Everyone.

5. Click OK to close the Permissions for Stuff dialog box. Click OK to close Advanced Sharing and then click Close to close the Stuff Properties dialog box.

6. Using File Explorer, open the \\contoso.com\NETLOGON folder.

7. Click the View menu and then select the File name extensions check box.

8. Take a screen shot of the NETLOGON window showing the File name extensions option window by pressing Alt+Prt Scr and then paste it into your Lab20_worksheet file in the page provided by pressing Ctrl+V.

9. Right-click the empty white part of the NETLOGON folder and choose New > Text Document. For the name, highlight the entire filename, type **MAP.bat** and then press Enter. Make sure that the filename extension is .bat, not .txt. If you are prompted to confirm that you want to change the extension, click Yes.

10. Right-click Map.bat and choose Edit. Notepad opens. When the warning displays, click Run.

> **NOTE** *You are asked to confirm that you want to run this file, but because you chose Edit instead of Run, the batch file will not be executed when you click Run.*

11. Type **net use g: \\Server01\Stuff**

12. In Notepad, click File > Exit. When you are prompted to save the changes, click Save.

13. On RWDC01, using Group Policy Management Editor for GP20, navigate to and click User Configuration\Policies\Windows Settings\Scripts (Logon/Logoff).

14. Double-click Logon to open the Logon Properties dialog box, as shown in Figure 20-3.

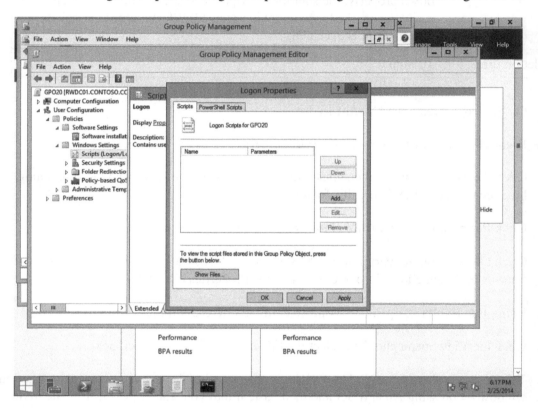

Figure 20-3
Configuring Logon scripts

15. Click Add to open the Add a Script dialog box.

16. In the Script Name text box, type **\\contoso\.com\NETLOGON\map.bat** and then click OK. Click OK to close the Logon Properties dialog box.

17. In the Group Policy Management Editor, open the Computer Configuration\Policies\Administrative Templates\System\Group Policy\ node and then double-click Configure Logon Script Delay. Select the Enabled check box.

Question 4	*What is the default delay before scripts are executed?*

18. Change the minutes to 1 minute.

19. Click OK to close the Configure Logon Scripts Delay dialog box.

20. Using the Group Policy Management console, right-click the Eng organizational unit and choose Group Policy Update. When you are prompted to confirm that you want to update the policy for these computers, click Yes.

21. While this may take a few minutes to finish replicating, on RWDC01, open Command Prompt (Admin), and then execute the following command to reboot Server02.

```
shutdown /m \\server02 /r /f
```

22. After Server02 reboots, log in as contoso\TReynolds with the password of Pa$$w0rd.

23. Open File Explorer and wait until the G drive is mapped.

End of exercise. Keep all servers logged in and leave the Group Policy Management Editor and the Command Prompt (Admin) windows open for the next exercise.

Exercise 20.4	Using Administrative Templates
Overview	In this exercise, you will configure the desktop wallpaper and screen saver settings. The screen saver settings are used to help protect a system by activating a screen saver when a user walks away from his or her computer for more than 15 minutes. If the screen saver is activated, the user will have to input his or her password to resume.
Mindset	Administrative Template policies contain registry-based policy settings that are used to configure the user and computer environment. For example, to configure the user's desktop image or a default screen saver, you use an Administrative Template policy. As you can imagine, there are hundreds of settings that are available.
Completion time	10 minutes

1. On RWDC01, using Group Policy Management Editor for GPO20, navigate to and click User Configuration\Policies\Administrative Templates\Desktop\Desktop.

2. Double-click Desktop Wallpaper. The Desktop Wallpaper dialog box opens.

3. Click Enabled. In the Wallpaper Name text box, type the following:

```
C:\Windows\Web\Screen\img101.png
```

4. Take a screen shot of the Desktop Wallpaper dialog box by pressing Alt+Prt Scr and then paste it into your Lab20_worksheet file in the page provided by pressing Ctrl+V.

5. Click OK to close the Desktop Wallpaper dialog box. The Desktop Wallpaper shows as Enabled.

6. Navigate to and click User Configuration\Policies\Administrative Templates\Control Panel\Personalization.

7. Double-click Enable screen saver. The Enable screen saver dialog box opens.

8. Click Enabled and then click OK to close the Enable screen saver dialog box.

9. Double-click Force specific screen saver. The Force specific screen saver dialog box opens.

10. Click Enabled. In the Screen Saver executable name, type **scrnsave.scr** and then click OK to close the Force specific screen saver.

11. In the Personalization node, double-click Screen saver timeout.

12. Click Enabled and then answer the following question.

Question 5	What is the default number of seconds?

13. Change the timeout to 120 seconds. Then click OK to close the Screen saver timeout dialog box.

14. Lastly, double-click Password protect the screen saver. The Password protect the screen saver dialog box opens.

15. Click Enabled. Click OK to close the Password protect the screen saver dialog box.

16. Take a screen shot of the Group Policy Management Editor showing the Personalization settings in the right pane by pressing Alt+Prt Scr and then paste it into your Lab20_worksheet file in the page provided by pressing Ctrl+V.

17. Close the Group Policy Management Editor window.

18. This may take a few minutes to finish replicating. On RWDC01, open a command prompt and then execute the following command to reboot Server02.

```
shutdown /m \\server01 /r /f
```

19. On Server02, log in as contoso\TReynolds with the password of Pa$$w0rd.

20. Do not press any keys on the keyboard or move the mouse on Server02. Wait at least 3 minutes to see the screensaver turn on.

21. Unlock the screensaver by logging in as contoso\TReynolds with the password of Pa$$w0rd.

End of exercise. Log off Server02.

Exercise 20.5	Using Security Templates
Overview	In this exercise, you will open a security template for domain controllers and use it to compare settings with RWDC01.
Mindset	Security templates include a list of GPO settings. You use them to make sure that a system is compliant with the settings saved in the template. After the template is created, you use Security Configuration and Analysis tool to compare the settings.
Completion time	10 minutes

1. On RWDC01, right-click the Start menu and choose Command Prompt (Admin).

2. At the command prompt, execute the mmc command. An empty console opens.

3. Click File > Add/Remove Snap-in.

4. When the Add or Remove Snap-ins dialog box opens, scroll down and click Security Templates. Click Add and then Click OK. The Security Templates snap-in is available.

5. Select the Security Templates snap-in in the left pane. Click Action > New Template Search Path. When the Browse For Folder dialog box opens, navigate to and click the following folder: C:\Windows\security\templates

6. Take a screen shot of the Console1 – [Console Root\Security Templates] windows and Browse For Folder dialog box by pressing Alt+Prt Scr and then paste it into your Lab20_worksheet file in the page provided by pressing Ctrl+V.

7. Click OK to close the Browse for Folder dialog box. In the MMC console, double-click C:\Windows\security templates and then double-click the DC security template.

8. Browse the various settings. Be sure to view the System Services.

9. Close the MMC console. When you are prompted to save the console, click No.

10. Back at the command prompt, execute the **mmc** command again. An empty console opens.

11. Click File > Add/Remove Snap-in.

12. When the Add or Remove Snap-ins dialog box opens, scroll down and click Security Configuration and Analysis. Click Add and then click OK. The Security Configuration and Analysis console is available.

13. In the left pane, Right-click Security Configuration and Analysis and choose Open Database. In the File name text box, type **Test** and then click Open.

14. When you are prompted to import the template, in the file name text box, type the following:

    C:\Windows\security\templates\DC security.inf

15. Right-click Security Configuration and Analysis and choose Analyze Computer Now. When the Perform Analysis dialog box opens, click OK.

16. When the analysis is done, check the settings looking for settings that are not compliant. Be sure to look at System Services.

17. Close the Security Configuration and Analysis console.

End of exercise.

LAB REVIEW QUESTIONS

Completion time	10 minutes

1. In Exercise 20.1, what type of programs can you install with a GPO?

2. In Exercise 20.1, when you deploy software with group policies, which option allows you to automatically install software when the user clicks the application icon or when a user tries to open a file that is associated with the specified application?

3. In Exercise 20.2, if you decide to redirect the Document folder, what other folder should you consider to redirect for users that might also have user documents?

4. In Exercise 20.3, list some of the types of scripts that you can execute with GPOs?

5. In Exercise 20.4, what is used to customize a user's Windows look and feel?

6. In Exercise 20.5, what is used to check security settings of a computer running Windows Server 2012?

Lab Challenge	Using ADM Files
Overview	To complete this challenge, you must demonstrate how to install and use the ADMX Migrator by writing the steps to complete the tasks described in the scenerio.
Mindset	You have an older ADM file used with GPOs. You need to convert the ADM file to an ADMX file so that you can use it with Windows Server 2012 R2 GPOs. Therefore, you must demonstrate how to install and use the ADMX Migrator.
Completion time	15 minutes

Write out the steps you performed to complete the challenge.

End of lab.

LAB 21
MANAGING GROUP POLICY OBJECTS

THIS LAB CONTAINS THE FOLLOWING EXERCISES AND ACTIVITIES:

Exercise 21.1   Backing Up and Restoring GPOs

Exercise 21.2   Importing and Copying GPOs

Exercise 21.3   Resetting Default GPOs

Exercise 21.4   Delegating Group Policy Management

Lab Challenge   Using a Migration Table

BEFORE YOU BEGIN

The lab environment consists of student workstations connected to a local area network, along with a server that functions as the domain controller for a domain called *contoso.com*. The computers required for this lab are listed in Table 21-1.

Table 21-1
Computers Required for Lab 21

Computer	Operating System	Computer Name
Server (VM 1)	Windows Server 2012 R2	RWDC01

In addition to the computers, you also require the software listed in Table 21-2 to complete Lab 21.

Table 21-2
Software Required for Lab 21

Software	Location
Lab 21 student worksheet	Lab21_worksheet.docx (provided by instructor)

Working with Lab Worksheets

Each lab in this manual requires that you answer questions, take screen shots, and perform other activities that you will document in a worksheet named for the lab, such as Lab21_worksheet.docx. You will find these worksheets on the book companion site. It is recommended that you use a USB flash drive to store your worksheets, so you can submit them to your instructor for review. As you perform the exercises in each lab, open the appropriate worksheet file using Word, fill in the required information, and save the file to your flash drive.

After completing this lab, you will be able to:

- Back up and restore GPOs

- Import and copy GPOs

- Reset the Default GPOs

- Delegate management of group policies

- Use a migration table

Estimated lab time: 60 minutes

Exercise 21.1	Backing Up and Restoring a GPO
Overview	In this exercise, you will back up several GPOs and then restore a single backed-up GPO.
Mindset	You should regularly back up the GPOs. You should also back up the GPOs before you make any major changes to them.
Completion time	10 minutes

1. Log in to Server01 as the Contoso\Administrator with the Pa$$w0rd password.

2. On Server01, create the C:\GPOBak folder.

3. Right-click the C:\GPOBak folder and choose Properties.

4. Click the Sharing tab and then click Advanced Sharing. The Advanced Sharing dialog box opens. Then click Share this folder.

5. Click Permissions. Click the Allow Full Control permission for Everyone.

6. Click OK to close the Permissions. Click OK again and then click Close to close the GPOBak Properties dialog box.

7. Log in to RWDC01 as the Contoso\Administrator user account. The Server Manager console opens.

8. On Server Manager, click Tools > Group Policy Management. The Group Policy Management console opens.

9. Navigate to and click the Group Policy Objects container.

Question 1	Before you make any major changes to a group policy, particularly the Default Domain Policy and Default Domain Controller Policy, what should you consider?

10. To back up all GPOs, right-click the Group Policy Object container and choose Back Up All. The Back Up Group Policy Object dialog box opens.

11. In the Location Text Box, type **\\server01\GPOBAK**. In the Description text box, type **GPO Backup <Today's Date>** and then click Back Up.

12. When the backup is complete, take a screen shot of the Backup dialog box by pressing Alt+Prt Scr and then paste it into your Lab21_worksheet file by pressing Ctrl+V.

13. When the backup is complete, click OK.

14. Expand Group Policy Objects.

15. Right-click Audit Policy and choose Back Up. In the Description, type **Audit Policy Backup <Today's Date>** and then click Back Up. When the backup is complete, click OK.

16. To restore a GPO, right-click the Audit Policy GPO and choose Restore from Backup.

17. When the Restore Group Policy Object Wizard opens, click Next.

18. On the Backup location page, click Next.

19. Choose the first Audit Policy backup and then click Next.

20. When the Restore GPO Wizard is complete, take a screen shot of the Restore Group Policy Object Wizard dialog box by pressing Alt+Prt Scr and then paste it into your Lab21_worksheet file by pressing Ctrl+V.

21. Click the Finish button.

22. When the restore is complete, click OK.

End of exercise. Leave the Group Policy Management console open for the next exercise.

Exercise 21.2	Importing and Copying GPOs
Overview	In this exercise, you will manage your GPOs by importing and copying GPOs.
Mindset	If you want to create a GPO that is similar to another GPO that you already have, you can either import the settings of the old GPO to the new GPO or simply copy the old GPO. Afterward, you can then modify the new policy and deploy as necessary.
Completion time	15 minutes

1. On RWDC01, using Group Policy Management, right-click the contoso.com node and choose Create a GPO in this domain, and Link it here.

2. When the New GPO dialog box opens, in the Name text box, type **GPO21a** and then click OK.

3. Right-click GPO21a and choose Edit. If a pop-up window opens, click OK. The Group Policy Management Editor opens.

4. Navigate to Computer Configuration\Policies\Administrative Templates\Control Panel\Personalization.

5. Double-click Prevent enabling lock screen camera.

6. When the Prevent enabling lock screen camera dialog box opens, click Enabled and then click OK.

7. Close Group Policy Management Editor.

8. Right-click the contoso.com node and choose Create a GPO in this domain, and Link it here.

9. When the New GPO dialog box opens, in the Name text box, type **GPO21b** and then click OK.

10. Navigate to and click the Group Policy Objects container.

11. To back up all GPOs, right-click the Group Policy Objects container and choose Back Up All. The Back Up Group Policy Object dialog box opens.

12. In the Location Text Box, \\Server01\GPOBAK should already be specified. Click Back Up.

13. When the backup is complete, click OK.

14. In the left pane, click the GPO21a. Then click the Settings tab to verify the current settings.

15. If an Internet Explorer message box opens, click Add on the Internet Explorer message box. Then click Add in Trusted sites dialog box, and click Close.

16. Right-click GPO21b and choose Import Settings.

17. When the Welcome screen opens, click Next.

18. On the Backup GPO page, click Next.

19. On the Backup location page, click Next.

20. Click the GPO21a and then click Next.

21. On the Scanning Backup page, click Next.

22. When the Import Settings Wizard is complete, click Finish.

23. When the import is complete, click OK.

24. To copy GPO21a, right-click GP021a and choose Copy.

25. Right-click the Group Policy Objects container and choose Paste.

26. When the Copy GPO dialog box appears, click Use the default permissions for new GPOs. Click OK.

27. When the copy is complete, click OK.

28. Right-click the copy of GPO21a and choose Rename. Type **GPO21c** and then press Enter.

29. Lastly, instead of always creating a new GPO, you can also link a container to a current GPO. For example, right-click the Domain Controllers container and choose Link an Existing GPO.

30. When the Select GPO dialog box opens, click GPO21a and then click OK.

31. Click GPO21a in the left pane. Click the Scope tab in right pane.

32. Take a screen shot of the Group Policy Management window by pressing Alt+Prt Scr and then paste it into your Lab21_worksheet file by pressing Ctrl+V.

Question 2	*What are the two OUs that GPO21a is linked to?*

End of exercise. Close the Group Policy Management console.

Exercise 21.3	Resetting Default GPOs
Overview	Probably the two most important GPOs are the default GPOs that come with Windows Server 2012. In this exercise, you will reset those GPOs.
Mindset	The Default Domain Policy has the default account policies and the Default Domain Controller Policy has the default User Rights Assignments.
Completion time	5 minutes

1. On RWDC01, right-click the Start menu and choose Command Prompt (Admin).

2. At the prompt, execute the **DcGPOFix** command.

3. When you are warned that you are about to restore the Default Domain Policy and Default Domain Controller Policy, type **Y** for Yes and then press Enter.

4. When you are prompted to confirm that you want to replace all User Rights Assignments, type **Y** for Yes and then press Enter.

End of exercise. Close the Administrator: Command prompt window.

Exercise 21.4	Delegating Group Policy Management
Overview	In this exercise, you will delegate permissions so that other users can either manage GPOs or create new GPOs.
Mindset	Group policies can be a powerful tool and they are essential to make an organization secure. In addition, because group policies are so powerful, you can cause a wide range of problems if you don't configure them properly.
Completion time	10 minutes

1. On RWDC01, with Server Manager, click Tools > Active Directory Users and Computers.

2. Right-click the Users node under contoso.com and choose New > User.

3. When the New Object – User dialog box opens, specify the following information and then click Next:

    First name: **Pete**

    Last name: **Russell**

    User logon name: **prussell**

4. For the Password text box and the Confirm password text box, type **Pa$$w0rd**. Click Password never expires. When the warning appears, click OK and then click Next.

5. Click Finish.

6. Close Active Directory Users and Computers.

7. With Server Manager, click Tools > Group Policy Management. The Group Policy Management console opens.

8. Navigate to and click the Group Policy Objects container.

9. Click the Delegation tab.

10. To specify who can create GPOs, click Add. When the Select User, Computer, or Group dialog box opens, type **Pete Russell** and then click OK.

Question 3	*A user creates a GPO. What do you need to do in order for that user to manage the GPO that he or she created?*

11. To specify who can manage an individual GPO, click GPO21c and then click the Delegation tab.

12. To add a user or group, click Add. When the Select User, Computer, or Group dialog box opens, in the Enter the object name to select text box, type **Pete Russell** and then click OK.

13. When the Add Group or User dialog box opens, set Pete's Permissions to Edit settings, delete, modify security and then click OK.

14. Take a screen shot of the Group Policy Management window (showing the Delegation tab for GPO21c) by pressing Alt+Prt Scr and then paste it into your Lab21_worksheet file by pressing Ctrl+V.

End of exercise. Close the Group Policy Management console.

LAB REVIEW QUESTIONS

Completion time	5 minutes

1. In Exercise 21.1, what tool is used to back up GPOs?

2. In Exercise 21.2, how many containers can a GPO be assigned to?

3. In Exercise 21.3, what command did you use to reset the default GPOs?

4. In Exercise 21.4, what tool is used to manage permissions of a GPO?

Lab Challenge	Using a Migration Table
Overview	To complete this challenge, you must use a Migration Table with a GPO with the following Mindset scenario.
Mindset	For your organization, you have several domains. The primary domain has most of the users and network resources. You also have a smaller test domain. You have a GPO that you have created and successfully tested on the test domain. You want to copy the GPO to the production GPO. What steps do you need to perform to use the GPO?
Completion time	15 minutes

Write out the steps you performed to complete the challenge.

End of lab.

LAB 22
CONFIGURING GROUP POLICY PREFERENCES

THIS LAB CONTAINS THE FOLLOWING EXERCISES AND ACTIVITIES:

Exercise 22.1   Configuring Printer Settings

Exercise 22.2   Configuring Network Drive Mappings

Exercise 22.3   Configuring Power Options

Exercise 22.4   Configuring Internet Explorer (IE) Settings

Exercise 22.5   Performing File, Folder, and Shortcut Deployment

Lab Challenge   Configuring Item-Level Targeting

BEFORE YOU BEGIN

The lab environment consists of student workstations connected to a local area network, along with a server that functions as the domain controller for a domain called *contoso.com*. The computers required for this lab are listed in Table 22-1.

Table 22-1
Computers Required for Lab 22

Computer	Operating System	Computer Name
Server (VM 1)	Windows Server 2012 R2	RWDC01
Server (VM 2)	Windows Server 2012 R2	Server01

In addition to the computers, you also require the software listed in Table 22-2 to complete Lab 22.

Table 22-2
Software Required for Lab 22

Software	Location
Lab 22 student worksheet	Lab22worksheet.docx (provided by instructor)

Working with Lab Worksheets

Each lab in this manual requires that you answer questions, take screen shots, and perform other activities that you will document in a worksheet named for the lab, such as Lab22_worksheet.docx. You will find these worksheets on the book companion site. It is recommended that you use a USB flash drive to store your worksheets, so you can submit them to your instructor for review. As you perform the exercises in each lab, open the appropriate worksheet file using Word, fill in the required information, and save the file to your flash drive.

After completing this lab, you will be able to:

■ Configure Group Policy preferences including printers, network drive mappings, power options, Internet Explorer settings, and file and folder deployment

■ Configure item-level targeting

Estimated lab time: 70 minutes

Exercise 22.1	Configuring Printer Settings
Overview	In this exercise, you will configure a local printer using GPO preferences.
Mindset	The key difference between preferences and policy settings is enforcement. Although group policies settings cannot be modified, GPP writes preferences to the same locations in the registry that the application or operating system feature uses to store the setting. Although the group policy setting interface is usually disabled or grayed out, preference settings can still be changed.
Completion time	10 minutes

1. Log in to Server01 as the Contoso\Administrator user account with the Pa$$w0rd password. The Server Manager console opens.

2. On Server01, right-click the Start button and choose Control Panel.

3. In the Control Panel, under Hardware, click View devices and printers,.

4. Click Add a printer and then click The printer that I want isn't listed.

5. Click Add a local printer or network printer with manual settings and then click Next.

6. On the Choose a printer port page, use the existing port that is already set to LPT1. Click Next.

7. Under the manufacturer, click HP. Under Printers, click LaserJet 6L PS Class Driver and then click Next.

8. On the Type a printer name page, click Next.

9. On the Printer Sharing, click Next.

10. When the wizard is complete, click Finish.

11. Log in to RWDC01 as the Contoso\Administrator user account with the Pa$$w0rd password. The Server Manager console opens.

12. On Server Manager, open Group Policy Management.

13. Right-click contoso.com and choose Create a GPO in this domain, and Link it here.

14. When the New GPO dialog box opens, type **GPO22** in the Name text box and then click OK.

15. Navigate to the Group Policy Objects container and click GPO22. If needed, click OK to close a message box that might appear. Then right-click GPO22 and choose Edit. The Group Policy Management Editor opens.

16. Navigate to and click Computer Configuration\Preferences\Control Panel Settings\Printers as shown in Figure 22-1.

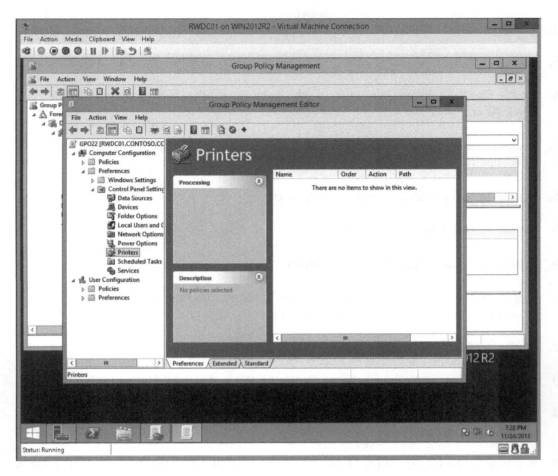

Figure 22-1
Configuring printers with preferences

17. Right-click the Printers node and choose New > Local Printer. The New Local Printer Properties dialog box opens.

18. For Action, Update is already selected. For the name, type **Office Printer**. For port, click USB001. For the Printer Path, type **\\Server01\HP LaserJet 6L PS Class Driver**.

19. Click OK. The new preference item appears in the Printers pane.

20. Take a screen shot of the Group Policy Management Editor window by pressing Alt+PrtScr and then paste it into your Lab22_worksheet file in the page provided by pressing Ctrl+V.

Question 1	*If you want to deploy a GPO based on where a user is located, where would you best assign the GPO?*

End of exercise. Leave Group Policy Management Editor open for the next exercise.

Exercise 22.2	Configuring Network Drive Mappings
Overview	In this exercise, you will map a shared folder to the local I drive.
Mindset	Network drive maps allow you to create dynamic drive mappings to network shares, modify mapped drives, delete a mapped drive, or hide or show drives.
Completion time	5 minutes

1. On RWDC01, using the Group Policy Management Editor for GPO22, navigate to and click User Configuration\Preferences\Windows Settings\Drive Maps.

2. Right-click the Drive Maps node and choose New > Mapped Drive. The New Drive Properties dialog box opens.

3. In the Location text box, type **\\Server01\Data**.

4. Under Drive Letter, select the I drive.

5. Under Hide/Show this drive, click Show this drive.

6. Take a screen shot of the New Drive Properties dialog box by pressing Alt+Prt Scr and then paste it into your Lab22_worksheet file in the page provided by pressing Ctrl+V.

7. Click OK to close the New Drive Properties dialog box.

End of exercise. Leave the Group Policy Management Editor open for the next exercise.

Exercise 22.3	Configuring Power Options
Overview	In this exercise, you will configure Power Options using GPO Preferences.
Mindset	The Power options extension allows you to create and configure Power Plan, Power Options, and Power Scheme preference items. The Power Options and Power Schemes are used with Windows XP and Windows Vista; Power Plan is used with Windows Vista and later.
Completion time	10 minutes

1. On RWDC01, using the Group Policy Management Editor for GPO22, navigate to and click Computer Configuration\Preferences\Control Panel Settings\Power Options.

2. Right-click the Power Options node and choose New > Power Plan (At least Windows 7). The New Power Scheme (At least Windows 7) Properties dialog box opens as shown in Figure 22-2.

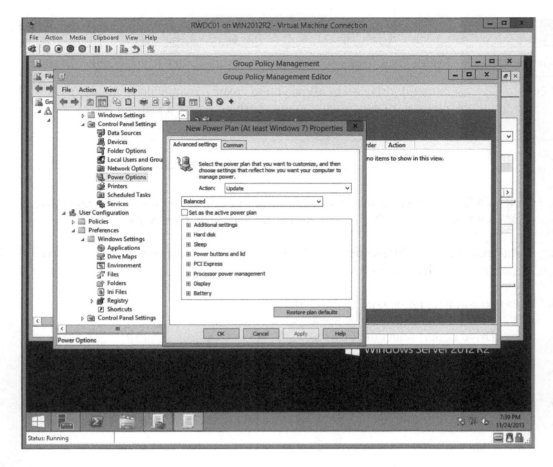

Figure 22-2
Creating a Power Plan

3. Expand Power buttons and lid, expand Lid close action, and then click Lid close action. Change the On battery and Plugged in setting from Sleep to Do nothing.

4. Expand Display and then expand Turn off display after.

Question 2	How long does it take before the display is turned off when the system is plugged in?

5. Click the Common tab.

6. Click Apply once and do not reapply.

7. Click OK to close the New Power Plan (At least Windows 7) Properties dialog box. The new preference item appears in the Power Options pane.

8. Take a screen shot of the Group Policy Management Editor window by pressing Alt+PrtScr and then paste it into your Lab22_worksheet file in the page provided by pressing Ctrl+V.

End of exercise. Leave the Group Policy Management Editor open for the next exercise.

Exercise 22.4	Configuring Internet Explorer (IE) Settings
Overview	In this exercise, you will configure Internet Explorer (versions 8 through 10) with a predefined home page and pop-up blocker exceptions.
Mindset	When you configure IE preference extensions, some of the options have a red dashed line under them. You have to toggle the editing state by pressing the F5 key to enable all or pressing F6 to enable current.
Completion time	15 minutes

1. On RWDC01, using the Group Policy Management Editor for GPO22, navigate to and click User Configuration\Preferences\Control Panel Settings\Internet Settings.

2. Right-click the Internet Settings node and choose New > Internet Explorer 10. The New Internet Explorer 10 Properties dialog box opens as shown in Figure 22-3.

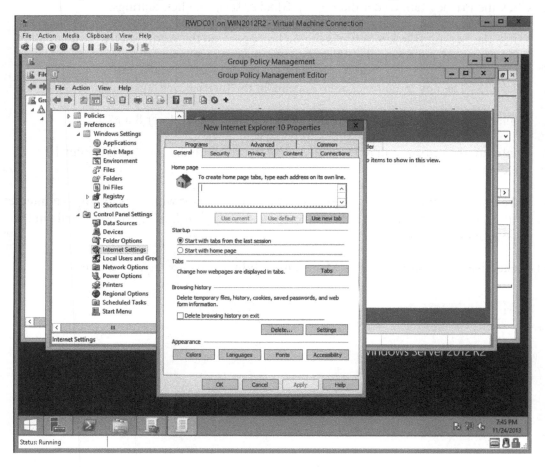

Figure 22-3
Configuring Internet Explorer 10 with preferences

3. On the General tab, in the Home page text box, type **http://portal.contoso.com**. Click Start with home page.

Question 3	What color is the home page set as?

Question 4	What color is the Startup options set as?

4. Click the Home page text box. Press the F5 key so that the box turns green.

Question 5	Which key is used to disable the current setting?

5. Click the Privacy tab. Under the Pop-up Blocker section, click Settings.

6. When the Pop-up Blocker Settings dialog box opens, in the Address of website to allow text box, type ***.contoso.com**. Click Add and then click Close.

7. Click OK. The new preference item appears in the Internet Settings pane.

8. Right-click Internet Settings and choose New > Internet Explorer 8 and 9.

9. Configure the setting similar to what you configured with the Internet Explorer 10 preference.

10. Take a screen shot of the Group Policy Management Editor window showing the Internet Settings by pressing Alt+Prt Scr and then paste it into your Lab22_worksheet file in the page provided by pressing Ctrl+V.

End of exercise. Leave Group Policy Management Editor open for the next exercise.

Exercise 22.5	Performing File, Folder, and Shortcut Deployment
Overview	In this exercise, you will create a folder, copy a file to the folder, and then create a shortcut to the folder using GPO Preferences.
Mindset	When you select Create, it creates a new preference setting for the user or computer. When you select Update, it modifies an existing preference setting for the user or computer. However, the Create option will create a file the next time the policy is applied if it is not already there. The Update setting will modify the file the next time the policy is applied and create the file if it does not exist.
Completion time	15 minutes

1. On RWDC01, using the Group Policy Management Editor for GPO22, navigate to and click User Configuration\Preferences\Windows Settings\Files.

2. Right-click the Files node and choose New > File. The New File Properties dialog box opens.

3. In the Source file(s) text box, type **\\server01\Stuff\Hello.bat**.

4. In the Destination File, click c:\hello.bat.

5. Take a screen shot of the New File Properties dialog box by pressing Alt+Prt Scr and then paste it into your Lab22_worksheet file in the page provided by pressing Ctrl+V.

6. Click OK to close the New File Properties dialog box.

7. Navigate to and click Computer Configuration\Preferences\Windows Settings\Folders.

8. Right-click the Folders node and choose New > Folder. The New Folder Properties dialog box opens.

9. For the Action, select Create. In the Path text box, type **C:\Batch**.

10. Click OK to close the New Folder Properties dialog box.

11. Navigate to and click User Configuration\Preferences\Windows Settings\Shortcuts.

12. Right-click the Shortcuts node and choose New > Shortcut. The New Shortcut Properties dialog box opens.

13. For the Action, select Create.

14. In the Name text box, type **Batch**.

15. Using the Location pull-down menu, select Desktop.

16. In the Target Path text box, type **C:\Batch**.

17. Click OK to close the New Shortcut Properties. The new preference item appears in the Shortcuts pane.

18. Close the Group Policy Management Editor.

End of exercise.

LAB REVIEW QUESTIONS

Completion time	5 minutes

1. In Exercise 22.1, what did you use to install and configure a printer?

2. In Exercise 22.2, what allows you to apply settings using a Group Policy once and then allow the user to change the settings in the future?

3. In Exercise 22.4, what key did you use to enable settings in IE settings?

4. In Exercise 22.5, you need to support IE 7, 8, 9 and 10. How many settings do you have to configure?

Lab Challenge	Configuring Item-Level Targeting
Overview	To complete this challenge, you must explain how to use Item-Level Targeting.
Mindset	You have preferences. How would you modify the GP022 so that it will affect only laptop computers?
Completion time	10 minutes

Explain the steps you would take to modify the GP022 settings so that it will affect only portable computers.

End of lab.